# Banking and Finance

Critical Infrastructure and Key Resources
Sector-Specific Plan as input to the
National Infrastructure Protection Plan

May 2007

 Homeland Security

 Department of the Treasury

**DEPARTMENT OF THE TREASURY**
WASHINGTON, D.C.

ASSISTANT SECRETARY

January 8, 2007

Mr. Robert B. Stephan
Assistant Secretary for Infrastructure Protection
Department of Homeland Security
Washington, D.C. 20528-0001

Dear Assistant Secretary Stephan:

As the Chair for the Financial and Banking Infrastructure Information Committee (FBIIC), I am please to transmit the Banking and Finance Sector Specific Plan (SSP). This plan was required by the Homeland Security Presidential Directive 7 and developed in accordance with guidance prepared by the Department of Homeland Security (DHS). The U.S. Department of the Treasury, as the Sector Specific Agency for the Banking and Finance Sector, developed this plan through close collaboration with the Federal and State financial regulators that comprise the FBIIC and with the private sector members of the Financial Services Sector Coordinating Council (FSSCC). Collectively, we received input from over 100 organizations representing all aspects of the sector.

The Banking and Finance SSP provides a strategy for working collaboratively with our public and private sector partners to identify the critical infrastructure and to prioritize and coordinate its protection. The plan summarizes sector activities already underway as well as additional efforts the sector will undertake to reduce vulnerabilities and share information.

It is the intention of the FBIIC that this SSP be included in the National Infrastructure Protection Plan, which provides the unifying structure for the integration of protection efforts across all 17 identified critical infrastructures and the Nation's key resources. The members of the FBIIC support the concepts and processes in this SSP and will continue to work with the Department of the Treasury and the FSSCC to implement the protective programs contained therein. Furthermore, the FBIIC members will continue to develop and maintain partnerships with appropriate Federal, State, regional, local, tribal, international, and nongovernmental entities. Additionally, the Department of the Treasury will continue to work with its security partners, including DHS to share information consistent with FBIIC members' agency-specific authorities and requirements.

We look forward to the final release of the National Infrastructure Protection Plan.

Sincerely,

Emil W. Henry, Jr.

# Financial Services Sector Coordinating Council
## for Critical Infrastructure Protection and Homeland Security

December 21, 2006

The Honorable Robert B. Stephan
Assistant Secretary for Infrastructure Protection
United States Department of Homeland Security
Washington, D.C. 20528

Dear Assistant Secretary Stephan:

I am writing on behalf of the Financial Services Sector Coordinating Council (FSSCC), the sector coordinating council for the Banking and Finance Sector, concerning the attached Sector Specific Plan (SSP) for our Sector. FSSCC has had ample opportunity to contribute to the SSP through discussions, reviews, opportunities to comment and meetings with the Department of the Treasury, the sector specific agency (SSA) for our Sector. Treasury took the lead in developing the SSP for our Sector in close collaboration with FSSCC and the Financial and Banking Information Infrastructure Committee (FBIIC).

FSSCC understands that the preparation of the SSP for our Sector is happening at the same time that SSPs are developed for the other 16 Sectors in order to implement the National Infrastructure Protection Plan (NIPP) for critical infrastructure and key resources (CI/KR). FSSCC hopes that preparation of the SSP for our Sector and the SSPs for the other 16 Sectors will result in the application of government resources to those areas where they offer the most benefit for mitigating risks by lowering vulnerabilities, deterring threats, and minimizing the consequences of attacks and other incidents. FSSCC encourages the risk-based allocation of resources within the private sector as well.

FSSCC supports the concepts and processes outlined in the SSP for our Sector, and will continue to work with Treasury and the other members of FBIIC to develop and implement the SSP. FSSCC has had the opportunity to provide insights and guidance on the unique needs, concerns, and perspectives of its members in the preparation of the SSP for our Sector. FSSCC plans to maintain partnerships for CI/KR protection with FBIIC and other appropriate Federal, State, regional, local, tribal and international entities as well as other private sector entities and non-governmental organizations. FSSCC will work with the Department of Homeland Security and Treasury to find suitable mechanisms to share CI/KR protection-related information.

Sincerely,

George Hender
Chairman, Financial Services Sector Coordinating Council

# Table of Contents

## List of Figures

## List of Tables

# Executive Summary

The Banking and Finance Sector accounts for more than 8 percent of the U.S. annual gross domestic product and is the backbone for the world economy. As direct attacks and public statements by terrorist organizations demonstrate, the sector is a high-value and symbolic target. Additionally, large-scale power outages, recent natural disasters, and a possible flu pandemic demonstrate the wide range of potential threats facing the sector. With this understanding, financial regulators and private sector owners and operators work collaboratively to maintain a high degree of resilience in the face of a myriad of potential disasters, be they intentional or unintentional, manmade or natural. This collaboration has led to a comprehensive framework for a strong public-private sector partnership. This partnership has developed several programs that currently provide protection and crisis management, which are continuously improving.

Working through this public-private partnership, the Department of the Treasury, as the Sector-Specific Agency (SSA) for the Banking and Finance Sector, has developed this Sector-Specific Plan (SSP) in close collaboration with the Financial and Banking Information Infrastructure Committee (FBIIC) and the Financial Services Sector Coordinating Council for Critical Infrastructure Protection and Homeland Security (FSSCC). This SSP, along with the SSPs from the 16 other critical infrastructures identified in Homeland Security Presidential Directive 7 (HSPD-7), are part of the overall National Infrastructure Protection Plan (NIPP). This SSP contains the Banking and Finance Sector's strategy for working collaboratively with public and private sector partners to identify, prioritize, and coordinate the protection of critical infrastructure. This SSP also summarizes the extensive activities the sector has undertaken already to reduce vulnerabilities and share information.

## 1. Sector Profile and Goals

The Banking and Finance SSP provides a description of the complex nature of the sector and an overview of the sector's provision of products and services, which are: (1) deposit, consumer credit, and payment systems; (2) credit and liquidity products; (3) investment products; and (4) risk-transfer products (including insurance).

Essential to this sector overview is a description of the Federal and State regulatory authorities as well as self-regulatory organizations. The Banking and Finance Sector is highly regulated with regulators providing oversight and, in some cases, guidance to and examinations of the financial institutions within their statutory purview. The financial regulators work together through the FBIIC to coordinate efforts with respect to critical infrastructure protection issues. In October 2001, the President established the FBIIC. The President's Working Group on Financial Markets currently sponsors the FBIIC, which is chaired by the Treasury Department's Assistant Secretary for Financial Institutions.

The private sector pillar of the security partnership is organized through the FSSCC, the Financial Services Information Sharing and Analysis Center (FS-ISAC), and the regional coalitions, which all promote voluntary information sharing efforts throughout the sector. The FSSCC membership is comprised of individual institutions, trade associations, and regional coalitions.

Collectively, its members control the majority of assets of the financial services sector. The FS-ISAC is the operational arm of the FSSCC, sharing specific information pertaining to physical and cyber threats, vulnerabilities, incidents, and potential protective measures and practices. The regional coalitions work to build relationships and share information among financial institutions and first responders, emergency management, and officials at the local level.

The public and private sectors share the following vision statement:

---

### Vision Statement for the Banking and Finance Sector

*To continue to improve the resilience and availability of financial services, the Banking and Finance Sector will work through its public–private partnership to address the evolving nature of threats and the risks posed by the sector's dependency upon other critical sectors.*

---

To meet this shared vision, the Banking and Finance Sector has three primary goals. As with all endeavors focused primarily on security, the goals form a triad of prevention, detection, and correction of harm:

1. To maintain its strong position of resilience, risk management, and redundant systems in the face of a myriad of intentional, unintentional, manmade, and natural threats;

2. To address and manage the risks posed by the dependency of the sector on the Communications, Information Technology, Energy, and Transportation sectors; and

3. To work with the law enforcement community, the private sector, and our international counterparts to increase the amount of available resources dedicated to tracking and catching criminals responsible for crimes against the sector, including cyber attacks and other electronic crimes.

The Banking and Finance Sector's efforts are supported by strong value propositions that address voluntary collaboration for both the public and private sectors. For the financial regulators, voluntary programs provide unique insights into sector-wide resilience efforts and allow for important information-sharing and risk management procedures outside traditional regulatory discussions and processes. These efforts provide a means for addressing dynamic risks through voluntary collaboration rather than solely through regulation.

For the private sector, the voluntary collaborative efforts provide institutions with the opportunity to gain unique insight into their regulators' perspectives and priorities. Most importantly, the private sector participates in voluntary efforts because of the concrete value they provide to their companies and, in turn, their customers.

## 2. Identify Assets, Systems, Networks, and Functions

The products offered by the Banking and Finance Sector are largely intangible. Thus, efforts to identify assets are largely focused on critical processes rather than physical assets. The FBIIC agencies, through their oversight authority and being shaped by 217 years of experience, obtain a vast amount of information on institutions, critical assets, and processes. These data are verified and updated through the continual process of regulatory examinations and mandated reporting.

## 3. Assess Risks

Risk assessments are a long-standing practice within the Banking and Finance Sector and accepted by both the regulators and the private sector. The Treasury Department and the FBIIC agencies meet continually with financial institutions to determine whether any new assets are critical to the operations of the sector and thus require special attention regarding potential vulnerabilities.

The Banking and Finance Sector assesses consequences based on whether the loss or impairment of an asset or process would impact the sector's ability to operate in an orderly and efficient manner. The sector participants also consider the potential impact on the public's confidence in the financial system as a whole. Through vulnerability assessments, the sector has determined that some of its greatest challenges are its dependency on telecommunications, the power grid, information technology, and transportation. Along with understanding vulnerabilities, the Banking and Finance Sector integrates threat analysis into its protective programs and shares threat information through the FBIIC and the FSSCC as necessary.

## 4. Prioritize Infrastructure

The Treasury Department, in conjunction with the FBIIC agencies and the private sector, identifies and prioritizes key infrastructures and updates this list annually. This prioritization is based on the impact to the orderly and efficient operation of the sector and public confidence if the infrastructure were no longer able to operate or were impaired. Factors for prioritization include: the degree of dependence on the asset; the presence or absence of alternatives to the infrastructure; the public need for the services provided by the asset; the potential impact of disruption to the financial system; and the potential impacts on the economy resulting from a cascading disruption of other critical infrastructures and key resources.

## 5. Develop and Implement Protective Programs

Both the public and private sectors have key roles to play in implementing protective programs. Through direct mandates and regulatory authority, financial regulators have specific regulatory tools that they may implement in response to a crisis. Additionally, the Treasury Department, along with the FBIIC agencies, the members of the FSSCC, the FS-ISAC, and the regional coalitions, have developed and begun implementing numerous protective programs to meet the stated security goals. These protective programs range from developing and testing robust emergency communication protocols to conducting and participating in a variety of exercises.

Successful programs already have been implemented, including sector-specific crisis communication facilities for events in progress, coordination of regional resources to mitigate known physical security threats, and coordination between regulatory and private sector organizations for pandemic planning. Protective programs still in progress include building formal information-sharing networks, subscribing to warning and alert systems, conducting targeted outreach, supporting the development of regional coalitions, and reaching out to other sector coordinating councils and law enforcement.

## 6. Measure Progress

The Treasury Department is working with our public and private sector partners to develop sector-specific metrics aligned with the sector security goals. The process for developing these metrics will incorporate collaboration and insights from sector participants, regulators, as well as other sectors' government and sector coordinating councils as appropriate. These include processes for developing metrics to address vulnerabilities stemming from gaps in sector dependencies, continuous improvement to the information-sharing framework, and unique challenges posed by cyber crime. The Treasury Department will coordinate with the FBIIC agencies and the FSSCC to validate, update, and implement these metrics.

Due to its complexity, measurements of the resilience efforts in the Banking and Finance Sector are difficult to quantify using standard business measurements. Therefore, a one-size-fits-all approach would be inapplicable to all aspects of the sector and also would weaken creativity and vitality in the sector, which would harm the Nation's economy overall.

## 7. CI/KR Protection Research & Development (R&D)

In 2006, the FSSCC formed a R&D Committee to develop plans and programs that would provide the most benefit to the specific critical infrastructure and key resources (CI/KR) requirements of the financial services sector. The R&D Committee has identified eight areas that present significant issues to the ability of the Banking and Finance Sector to meet its challenges: (1) Secure Financial Transaction Protocol (SFTP); (2) Resilient Financial Transaction System (RFTS); (3) enrollment and identity credential management; (4) suggested practices and standards; (5) understanding and avoiding the insider threat; (6) financial information tracing and policy enforcement; (7) testing; and (8) standards for measuring return on investment of critical infrastructure protection and security technology.

Accordingly, the R&D Committee views the following three themes to have the greatest impact to the financial services sector in terms of R&D projects: (1) protection and prevention systems; (2) advanced infrastructure architecture; and (3) human and social issues.

## 8. Managing and Coordinating SSA Responsibilities

The Secretary of the Treasury designated the Assistant Secretary for Financial Institutions as the Treasury official with the responsibility for carrying out the Treasury's duties as the SSA for the Banking and Finance Sector. The Assistant Secretary designated the Office of Critical Infrastructure Protection and Compliance Policy (OCIP) to provide the necessary functions on a daily basis. As such, the OCIP is the lead for all SSP activities and will continue to work with the FBIIC agencies and the FSSCC to coordinate any necessary updates and implementation efforts in conjunction with the triennial review of the National Infrastructure Protection Plan (NIPP) Base Plan.

Additionally, the Treasury Department will work with the FBIIC agencies and the FSSCC to provide any necessary training on the SSP, as well as training and education on business continuity, information sharing, emergency response protocols, and cross-sector dependencies.

Fortunately for the Banking and Finance Sector, a robust public-private sector partnership is already in place. The Treasury Department will continue to facilitate this partnership through our daily activities, outreach efforts, sponsoring of exercises, and through regularly scheduled meetings with the FBIIC and the FSSCC. The Treasury Department will continue to support and facilitate information-sharing efforts through the FBIIC, the FSSCC, the FS-ISAC, and regional coalitions.

# Introduction

According to Homeland Security Presidential Directive 7 (HSPD-7),[1] signed by the President on December 17, 2003, the Department of the Treasury, as the Sector-Specific Agency (SSA) for the Banking and Finance Sector, is required to develop a Sector-Specific Plan (SSP) for critical infrastructure protection. This SSP provides the Banking and Finance Sector's strategy for working collaboratively with public and private sector partners to identify, prioritize, and coordinate the protection of critical infrastructure. This SSP also summarizes the extensive activities the sector has already undertaken to reduce vulnerabilities and share information.

The Banking and Finance SSP is part of the overall National Infrastructure Protection Plan (NIPP). As such, the Banking and Finance SSP conforms to the guidance provided by Department of Homeland Security so that the Banking and Finance SSP may be included in the NIPP. The NIPP provides the structure for integration of this SSP and the SSPs of the other 16 critical infrastructures and key resources identified in HSPD-7, thereby bringing together the efforts of these sectors into a single national program.

---

[1] Homeland Security Presidential Directive 7 (HSPD-7), December 17, 2003, www.whitehouse.gov/news/releases/2003/12/20031217-5.html.

# 1. Sector Profile and Goals

The United States financial services sector is the backbone of the world economy. With assets estimated to be in excess of $48 trillion,[2] this large and diverse sector accounted for more than $900 billion in 2005 or 8.1 percent of the United States gross domestic product (GDP).[3] Descriptions of the sector's profile and goals necessarily include the diversity of its institutions and the services they provide. Most important to this profile is the understanding that the financial services sector is primarily owned and operated by the private sector whose institutions are extensively regulated by Federal and, in many cases, State government. In addition to these public sector entities, self-regulatory organizations (SROs), such as the Municipal Securities Rulemaking Board (MSRB), NASD, and the National Futures Association (NFA), and exchanges, such as the Chicago Mercantile Exchange (CME), the New York Stock Exchange (NYSE), and designated futures exchanges also play an important role in industry oversight.

The financial services sector is complex and diverse. From the largest institutions with assets greater than one trillion dollars to the smallest community banks and credit unions, this diversity provides the ability for the sector as whole to meet the needs of its large and diverse customer base. Whether it is an individual savings account, financial derivatives, credit extended to a large corporation, or investments made by a foreign country, financial institutions provide a broad array of products. These products: (1) allow customers to deposit funds and make payments to other parties (more than $12 trillion in assets);[4] (2) provide credit and liquidity to customers (more than $14 trillion in assets); (3) allow customers to invest funds for both long and short periods (more than $18 trillion in assets); and (4) transfer financial risks between customers (more than $6 trillion in assets).[5]

Despite this diversity, a unifying mission of the U.S. financial sector is to ensure the continued efficiency in and continuity of the sector and its institutions. Through the extensive regulatory regime and formalized information-sharing organizations detailed in this plan, the sector has wide-ranging transparency and accountability, which ensures an orderly and efficient financial system that serves a broad range of needs for both investors and consumers. In turn, these factors create a sense of confidence that enables customers to entrust their assets to the care of financial institutions and to avail themselves of credit and liquidity.

As this plan details, today's U.S. financial regulatory regime consists of both Federal and State agencies, whose oversight assists in ensuring the integrity of individual institutions and the overall U.S. financial system. Working together, the public and private sectors encourage a highly competitive market where identifying and managing a myriad of financial and non-financial risks is essential to success. Through numerous laws enacted by Congress over the past 150 years, Federal financial regulators have implemented a complex regime that in many instances provides for examinations of institutions' operational, financial,

---

[2] www.financialservicesfacts.org/financial2/today/assets.

[3] GDP in 2005, www.bea.gov/bea/dn2/gdpbyind_data.htm.

[4] www.fdic.gov/bank/statistical/stats/2e05dec/industry.html.

[5] www.federalreserve.gov/releases/Z1/20060309/Coded/coded-4.pdf.

and technological systems. These examinations are designed to determine the extent to which the institution has identified its financial and non-financial risks, such as information technology infrastructures, and to evaluate the adequacy of controls and applicable risk management practices at the institution.

Additionally, financial regulators update guidance to financial institutions regularly. This guidance assists the sector in staying abreast of the evolving nature of both financial and non-financial risks. Financial risk guidance addresses a variety of issues including credit risk, reinvestment risk, interest rate risk, currency risk, and others. Guidance on non-financial risks addresses potential means for increasing risk management and resilience in the face of potential impacts that may result from a terrorist attack, natural disaster, or other incident. To the extent possible, these regulators have identified critical vulnerabilities, whether they are financial or operational, including Internet and information technology vulnerabilities. (See appendix 2 for a list of statutory authorities and examples of regulators' examination tools and guidance.)

Furthering the Nation's ability to respond appropriately to and manage terrorism related risks, the President issued Homeland Security Presidential Directive 7 (HSPD-7). Among its primary objectives, HSPD-7 designates SSAs to lead collaborative efforts for the critical infrastructures. The Treasury Department is the SSA for the Banking and Finance Sector. As the SSA, the Treasury Department works with all relevant Federal departments and agencies, State, local and tribal governments, and the private sector, including key persons and entities in the financial services sector, to coordinate efforts to improve the sector's ability to prepare, respond, prevent, and mitigate against terrorism, natural disasters, and other intentional or unintentional risks.

The Treasury Assistant Secretary for Financial Institutions implements the Treasury Department's responsibilities under HSPD-7. As part of fulfilling the responsibilities outlined in HSPD-7, the Assistant Secretary chairs the Financial and Banking Information Infrastructure Committee (FBIIC). The FBIIC is the working group comprised of the Federal financial regulators and agencies and State financial regulatory trade associations. Through the FBIIC, the Assistant Secretary coordinates certain policies, procedures and responses to crises for the Federal and State financial regulators. (See section 1.2 for further details.)

To meet objectives set forth by HSPD–7 for collaboration with the private sector, the Treasury Department also works closely with the Financial Services Sector Coordinating Council for Critical Infrastructure Protection and Homeland Security (FSSCC). The FSSCC serves as the primary means for public-private sector collaboration and coordination. Members of the FSSCC include trade associations and financial institutions from all components of the private sector. Furthermore, the Secretary of the Treasury designates the private sector coordinator who, as a matter of practice, has been selected by the financial services industry to serve as the chair of the FSSCC. (See section 1.2 for further details.)

Along with the FSSCC, the Treasury Department supports the Financial Services Information Sharing and Analysis Center (FS-ISAC) and provides ongoing support of regional coalitions. (See section 1.2 for further details.)

## 1.1 Sector Profile

The Banking and Finance Sector is a service-based industry providing a wide variety of financial services in the United States, and many such services throughout the world. These services range from the simple cashing of a check to highly complex arrangements that facilitate the transferring of financial risks. Financial institutions are organized and regulated based on the services the institutions provide. Therefore, the sector profile is best described by defining the services offered. These categories include: (1) deposit and payment systems and products; (2) credit and liquidity products; (3) investment products; and (4) risk-transfer products.

With more than 17,000 depository institutions,[6] 15,000 providers of various investment products,[7] more than 8,500 providers of risk-transfer products,[8] and many thousands of credit and financing organizations, the financial services sector is both large in assets and in the number of individual businesses.

### 1.1.1 Deposit, Consumer Credit, and Payment Systems Products

Depository institutions of all types (banks, thrifts, and credit unions) are the primary providers of wholesale and retail payments services, such as wire transfers, checking accounts, and credit and debit cards. These institutions use and/or operate the payments infrastructure, which includes electronic large value transfer systems, Automated Clearinghouses (ACH), and automated teller machines (ATM). These institutions are the primary point of contact with the sector for many individual customers. Additionally, these institutions may be Federal or State-chartered banks or credit unions; however, in most instances, the Federal financial regulators have at least some authority over these institutions.

Along with the aforementioned payment systems, these depository institutions provide customers with various forms of extensions of credit, such as mortgages and home equity loans; collateralized and uncollateralized loans; and lines of credit, including credit cards. Consumers have multiple ways of accessing these services. For example, customers can make deposits in person at a depository institution's branch office, through the mail, at an ATM, or via direct deposit using ACH transactions. Customers can make withdrawals at a branch office, at an ATM, or by using a debit card or check. Customers also can access credit lines through other retail banking services using the telephone or the Internet. In the United States, customers typically have deposit, checking, and loan accounts with more than one depository institution. The average household may have up to 18 account relationships spread among 12 financial institutions.[9]

### 1.1.2 Credit and Liquidity Products

Customers seek liquidity and credit for a wide variety of needs. For example, individuals may seek a mortgage to purchase a home, businesses may obtain a line of credit to expand their operations, and governments may issue sovereign debt obligations. Many financial institutions, such as depository institutions, finance and lending firms, securities firms, and Government-Sponsored Enterprises (GSE) meet customers' long- and short-term needs through a multitude of financial products. Some of these entities provide credit directly to the end customer, while others do so indirectly by providing wholesale liquidity to those financial services firms that provide these services on a retail basis.

Essential to the credit and liquidity market is the assurance that these products are available with integrity and fairness. The law provides for consumer protections against fraud involving these products, as well as certain other consumer protections, many of which are tied directly to the specific type of credit and liquidity product. Furthermore, credit and liquidity products are governed by a complex body of laws. These laws include Federal and State securities laws, banking laws, and laws that are tailored to the specifics of a particular class of lending activity.

### 1.1.3 Investment Products

A strong investment environment is essential to the growth of the U.S. economy. Moreover, the diversity of investment service providers and products ensures that U.S. financial markets are the best in the world. These products provide opportunities for both short- or long-term investments and include debt securities (such as bonds and bond mutual funds) and equities (such as stocks or stock mutual funds), and derivatives (such as options and futures). Securities firms, depository institutions, pension funds, and GSEs all offer financial products that are used for investing needs. These investment products are issued and traded

---

6  www2.fdic.gov/sod/sodSumReport.asp?barItem=3&sInfoAsOf=2006 and www.ncua.gov/data/FOIA/foia.html.

7  www.icifactbook.org/06_fb_sec1.html.

8  National Association of Insurance Commissioners, 2004 *Insurance Department Resources Report*, p. 46.

9  *Sheshunoff Bank Profit Improvement Manual*.

in various organized markets, from physical trading floors to electronic markets. Certain securities—U.S. Treasuries and equities of some multinational companies—are traded around the globe 24 hours a day. The Treasury, the Securities and Exchange Commission (SEC), the Commodity Futures Trading Commission (CFTC), banking regulators, and insurance regulators all provide financial regulation for certain investment products. The SEC and CFTC have legally designated SROs. Notably, the SEC has the power to delegate authority to its SROs, national stock exchanges and NASD, to enforce certain industry standards and requirements related to securities trading and brokerage. Similarly, the CFTC oversees exchanges and the industry SRO, i.e., designated futures exchanges, and the NFA, which have regulatory authority to enforce industry standards and requirements related to futures trading and participants. These regulatory requirements are directed toward consumer protection, fair and orderly markets, and the ongoing capability of financial services firms to meet their financial obligations.

### 1.1.4 Risk-Transfer Products (Including Insurance)

The transfer of financial risks, such as the financial loss due to theft or the destruction of physical or electronic property resulting from a fire, cyber attack, or other loss event, or the loss of income due to a death or disability in a family, is an important tool for the sustainability of businesses and economic vitality of individuals and their families. A wide variety of financial institutions provide risk-transference products to meet this market need.

The U.S. market for financial risk-transfer products is among the largest in the world, measuring in the trillions of dollars. These products range from straightforward to exceedingly complex. For example, insurance companies, futures firms, and forwards participants offer financial products that allow customers to transfer various types of financial risks under a myriad of circumstances. Marketplace efficiency often requires that market participants engage in both financial investments as well as in financial risk transfers that enable risk hedging. Financial derivatives, including futures and security derivatives, can provide both of these functions for market participants.

### 1.1.5 Federal and Self-Regulation of Financial Services Firms

All financial services firms are subject to the discipline of the financial market, and these markets have strong, though often informal, market discipline and self-regulation. Many of these financial firms are subject to additional governmental and legally mandated regulation and self-regulation. Such regulation is designed to provide reasonable assurance that consumers are protected and that the financial services firm is able to meet its financial obligations on an ongoing basis.

### 1.1.6 State Regulation of Financial Services Firms

Some financial services may be regulated at both the Federal and State levels. Insurance services are unique in that they are primarily regulated by States. Under the McCarran-Ferguson Act of 1945,[10] Congress affirmed the exclusive right of the States to regulate the insurance industry. Except for a few Federal laws and regulations, State insurance commissioners generally have regulatory authority over all aspects of a firm's business, including rates and terms of policies, qualifications for licensing, market conduct, and financial structures and practices. (See appendix 2 for a listing of State statutory authorities.)

The chief insurance regulatory officials from each State collaborate through the National Association of Insurance Commissioners (NAIC). The NAIC is a member of the FBIIC. Many of the State insurance regulators review the disaster response and business continuity plans of insurers and conduct periodic examinations of these plans. Some States, such as New York, also are doing stress-testing of insurer plans following an event. This helps regulators be certain that the insurers are ready to serve their policyholders when disaster strikes. The NAIC developed a handbook for State insurance regulatory response to disasters entitled, *The State Disaster Response Plan*.

---

[10]  15 U.S.C. § 1011 et seq.

In addition to the insurance industry, State agencies regulate State-chartered banks, thrifts, and credit unions. Membership in the Federal Reserve System is optional for State-chartered banks, but all of the banks are insured by the Federal Deposit Insurance Corporation (FDIC). The Office of Thrift Supervision (OTS) also regulates State- chartered savings associations with FDIC insured deposits. The National Credit Union Administration (NCUA) may regulate State-chartered credit unions that have Federal deposit insurance. State agencies also regulate the purchase and sale of securities and the provision of investment advice regarding securities.

## 1.2 Security Partners

As the SSA for the Banking and Finance Sector, the Treasury Department recognizes the vital role of both the financial regulators and the private sector. These regulators and the private sector are committed to the Banking and Finance Sector's security partnership. Working collaboratively, this partnership achieves its security goals and addresses the evolving nature of the sector and its potential risks.

The Treasury Department has formalized the collaboration of the sector's regulators, associations, and individual market participants through the FBIIC, the FSSCC, and the FS-ISAC, as well as an increasing number of regional coalitions. These organizations are the recognized structures through which public and private financial services sector participants: (1) share information both at the national and local levels; (2) assess and mitigate sector-wide risks; (3) develop and maintain key relationships; (4) conduct periodic testing of emergency protocols to be used during times of crisis; (5) establish research priorities; (6) organize and conduct exercises; and (7) act as a focal point for information sharing between the public and private sectors.

Furthermore, the Treasury Department works closely with the Department of Homeland Security (DHS) to meet the sector's security objectives. As a member of various key working groups led by, the Treasury Department apprises DHS of situational priorities and remains fully engaged with DHS. Some of these working groups include the Information Technology Government Coordinating Council (IT GCC), the Emergency Support Function Leader Group (ESFLG), the Homeland Security Integrated Intelligence Board (HIIB RFI) Task Force, the Infosec Research Council (IRC), the National Cyber Response Coordination Group (NCRCG), the Strategic Homeland Infrastructure Risk Assessment (SHIRA), and the Cyber Security and Information Assurance (CSIA).

### 1.2.1 Relationships with Federal and State Regulators and Related Associations

In October 2001, the President established the FBIIC.[11] The President's Working Group on Financial Markets currently sponsors the FBIIC, which is chaired by the Treasury Department's Assistant Secretary for Financial Institutions. The FBIIC's role is to coordinate the efforts of Federal and State financial regulators with respect to critical infrastructure issues, including preparation for and response to cyber or physical attacks against the financial system or indirect attacks or events that may impact the sector. The FBIIC's membership includes experienced regulators from the following agencies and associations:

---

[11] Executive Order 13231, 66 Federal Register (FR) 53063 (2001).

Figure 1-1: FBIIC Members

| FBIIC Members |
|---|
| Commodity Futures Trading Commission (CFTC) |
| Conference of State Bank Supervisors (CSBS) |
| Farm Credit Administration (FCA) |
| Federal Deposit Insurance Corporation (FDIC) |
| Federal Housing Finance Board (FHFB) |
| Federal Reserve Bank of New York (FRBNY) |
| Federal Reserve Board (FRB) |
| National Association of Insurance Commissioners (NAIC) |
| National Association of State Credit Union Supervisors (NASCUS) |
| Office of the Comptroller of the Currency (OCC) |
| Office of Federal Housing Enterprise Oversight (OFHEO) |
| Office of Thrift Supervision (OTS) |
| Securities of Exchange Commission (SEC) |
| Securities Investor Protection Corporation (SIPC) |
| The Homeland Security Council (HSC) |
| U.S. Department of the Treasury |

These agencies have regulatory authority over different sections of the financial services sector and currently address infrastructure protection issues through routine regulatory interactions.

In fulfilling its mission, the FBIIC:

• Identifies critical infrastructure assets and their locations, and prioritizes their importance to the financial system;

- Establishes secure communications capability and protocols for communicating during an emergency among the financial regulators;

- Ensures that sufficient staff exist at each member agency with appropriate security clearances to handle classified information and coordinate in the event of an emergency;

- Encourages the private sector to conduct voluntary testing to improve emergency preparedness of critical financial institutions;

- Identifies the critical interdependencies of the Banking and Finance Sector with the Energy, Transportation, Communications, and Information Technology sectors; and

- Promotes information sharing among and between the Federal, State, local, and tribal authorities, as well as the private sector.

The Treasury Department also works with Federal, State, local, and tribal law enforcement, including DHS and the Department of Justice (DOJ). Areas in which collaborative initiatives are being undertaken include the following:

- Fighting financial crimes, such as fraud and identity theft; and cyber crimes, such as phishing, directed at financial institutions;[12]

- Providing protective-response planning exercises designed to protect key assets and critical infrastructures and create a response plan that incorporates State, local, and tribal law enforcement; and

- Enhancing communications and coordination across the sector.

As noted previously, these agencies have extensive means to identify, assess, and assist with mitigating risks at the institutions within their legal purview. (See appendix 2, "Public Sector Regulatory Tools, Guidance, and Reports," for specific examples from these agencies.) Specifically, these agencies include, but are not limited to, authority over the following components of the financial sector markets:

- The Bureau of the Public Debt administers the auction rules for Treasury marketable securities and the Government Securities Act regulations for participants in the secondary market for U.S. Government securities;

- The CFTC regulates futures commission merchants, introducing brokers, commodity trading advisors, commodity pool operators, futures markets, and derivatives clearing organizations. This is done in conjunction with exchanges such as the CME and the New York Mercantile Exchange, and the industry SRO, the NFA;

- The CSBS members regulate State-chartered banks;

- The FCA regulates the Farm Credit System;

- The FDIC regulates State-chartered banks that are not members of the Federal Reserve System and insured State branches of foreign banks;

- The FHFB regulates the Federal Home Loan Banks;

- The FRB regulates financial and bank holding companies and State-chartered member banks within the Federal Reserve System;

- The NAIC assists State insurance regulators in achieving their goals;

- Members of the NASAA represent State securities regulators;

---

[12] "Phishing" is a fraudulent scheme where an e-mail directs its recipients to Web sites where they are asked to provide confidential personal or financial information. Reports of phishing attacks rose dramatically in the last year.

- The NCUA regulates Federally chartered credit unions and shares some supervision responsibility with the State Supervisory Authorities for the Federally insured State-chartered credit unions;

- The OCC regulates national banks and the Federal branches and agencies of foreign banks;

- The OFHEO regulates Fannie Mae and Freddie Mac;

- The OTS regulates savings associations and savings and loan holding companies;

- The SEC regulates investment companies, investment advisors, broker-dealers, transfer agents, securities markets, and securities clearing organizations. This is done in conjunction with SROs such as MSRB, NASD, and NYSE;

- State insurance commissioners regulate insurance companies and producers; and

- The Treasury Department develops the Administration's economic and financial services sector policies.

## 1.2.2  Relationships with Private Sector Owner/Operators and Organizations

The Treasury Department has formed a strong bond with the private sector through the FSSCC, the FS-ISAC, and the regional coalitions. Members of these private sector organizations include depository and lending institutions, as well as exchanges, trade associations, and other organizations within the sector. The Treasury Department also consults individually with these institutions on the development or implementation of various policies, such as enhancing the sector's resilience.

### FSSCC

Under the auspices of the FBIIC, the Treasury facilitated the creation of the FSSCC in June 2002 as the private sector arm of its protection strategy. The Treasury Department designates the Sector Coordinator for the Banking and Finance Sector, who as a matter of practice, is chosen by the FSSCC to be the chair of the FSSCC. The FSSCC, whose membership represents the sector through financial trade associations and organizations, fosters and facilitates the coordination of sector-wide financial services voluntary initiatives to improve critical infrastructure protection and homeland security. The organizations comprising the FSSCC hold the majority of the assets of the financial services sector and include financial institutions, trade associations, and regional partnerships. The FSSCC's success is due to the strong commitment of its members and their significant time contribution by high-level executives who are focused on problem solving and driven by achievable outcomes. The following institutions and organizations are members of the FSSCC:

Figure 1-2: FSSCC Members

| FSSCC Members | |
|---|---|
| America's Community Bankers | Independent Community Bankers of America |
| American Bankers Association | Investment Company Institute |
| American Council of Life Insurers | Managed Funds Association |
| American Society for Industrial Security International | NACHA - The Electronic Payments Association |
| BAI | National Association of Federal Credit Unions |
| BITS/The Financial Services Roundtable | National Futures Association |
| ChicagoFIRST | New York Board of Trade |
| Chicago Mercantile Exchange | Securities Industry Association |
| CLS Group | Securities Industry Automation Corporation |
| Consumer Bankers Association | The Bond Market Association |
| Credit Union National Association | The Clearing House |
| Fannie Mae | The Depository Trust & Clearing Corporation |
| Financial Information Forum | The NASDAQ Stock Market, Inc. |
| Financial Services Information and Sharing and Analysis Center (FS-ISAC), LLC | The Options Clearing Corporation |
| Financial Services Technology Consortium | Visa USA & Visa International |
| Futures Industry Association | |

The mission of the FSSCC is to:

- Provide broad industry representation for critical infrastructure protection and homeland security (CIP/HLS) and related matters for the financial services sector and for voluntary sector-wide partnership efforts;

- Foster and promote coordination and cooperation among participating sector constituencies on CIP/HLS-related activities and initiatives;

- Identify voluntary efforts where improvements in coordination can foster sector preparedness for CIP/HLS;

- Establish and promote broad sector activities and initiatives that improve CIP/HLS, such as addressing interdependencies among the financial and other sectors;

- Identify barriers and recommend initiatives to improve the sharing of information and knowledge among the financial services sector; and

- Improve sector awareness of CIP/HLS issues, sector activities/initiatives, and opportunities for improved coordination.

The Treasury Department also works with private sector institutions by conducting response planning exercises. These exercises, which in the past have included law enforcement, Government, and intelligence agencies, coordinate response and communication among Federal, State, local, and tribal first responders to specific institutions.

The joint successes of the FBIIC and the FSSCC include the following:

- Suggestions for financial institutions for different threat conditions under the Homeland Security Advisory System. This document was originally developed by FSSCC members BITS and Securities Industry Association (SIA);

- Exchange of information and best practices for critical infrastructure protection issues;

- Post-incident analysis of cyber attacks and other disruptive events, such as the Northeast Blackout of 2003 and Hurricane Katrina in 2005, to improve Government and private sector remediation and response;

- Development of an integrated set of crisis management calls and actions across the sector; and

- Several protective response exercises with the private sector to improve public and private emergency preparedness of critical financial institutions.

### FS-ISAC

The Treasury Department also works closely with the FS-ISAC,[13] one of the oldest private information-sharing initiatives in the United States. The FS-ISAC was set up as the financial sector response to the requirements of Presidential Decision Directive 63 (Protecting America's Critical Infrastructures) in May 1998.

The mission of the FS-ISAC, in collaboration with the Treasury Department and the FSSCC, is to enhance the ability of the financial services sector to prepare for and respond to cyber and physical threats, and vulnerabilities and incidents, and to serve as the primary communications channel for the sector.

The FS-ISAC is the designated operational arm of the FSSCC and supports the protection of the U.S. financial services sector by providing assistance to both the FSSCC and the Treasury to identify, prioritize, and coordinate the protection of critical financial services, infrastructure service, and key resources; and to facilitate sharing of information pertaining to physical and cyber threats, vulnerabilities, incidents, and potential protective measures and practices.

The FS-ISAC has identified the following strategic objectives to accomplish its mission:

- Provide an effective forum for information sharing within the financial services sector, with other critical infrastructure and key resources (CI/KR) organizations, and with the U.S. Government;

- Identify critical financial services sector operational support issues and requirements and articulate those to the Treasury and DHS;

---

[13] As outlined in the National Strategy to Secure Cyberspace (February 2003), information sharing and analysis centers (ISACs) are the cornerstone of industry information sharing, www.whitehouse.gov/pcipb.

- Serve as the sector communications hub conveying timely and accurate cyber and physical threat information, and vulnerability and incident alerts to the membership;

- Serve as the sector communications hub during emergencies, through the delivery of rapid notifications and communications to and among the FS-ISAC and the FSSCC members;

- Identify and implement new services that add value to the membership and support the mission of the FS-ISAC; and

- Collaborate with the Treasury and the FSSCC to:

  - Foster awareness of the benefits of information sharing within the sector, among other CI/KR organizations, and within the Government;

  - Educate the financial services sector on key infrastructure protection issues, vulnerabilities, threats, risk management, and compliance issues; and

  - Coordinate with other public and private sector CI/KR organizations to ensure sector awareness and emergency preparedness.

The FS-ISAC is also a member of the ISAC Council, which fosters collaboration and sharing of information with the other critical infrastructure sectors.

In 2003 and 2004, the Treasury Department acquired $2 million in services from the FS-ISAC, which had the added benefit of enhancing the FS-ISAC's capabilities. The enhanced FS-ISAC now has the capacity to better serve the financial services sector. The FS-ISAC integrates physical and cyber threat information and provides a state-of-the-art technology platform for the confidential exchange of information.

## Regional Partnerships

The resilience of the financial services sector is enhanced by efficient and effective collaborative efforts of sector participants. The FBIIC and the FSSCC form a public-private partnership at the national level, and they ably address CIP/HLS issues that cut across most, if not all, of the financial sector. However, natural and manmade disasters occur locally. Enhancing and maintaining the resilience of financial institutions in the face of a crisis thus depends upon the following:

- How well the business continuity and security plans of institutions incorporate emergency response and recovery measures of police, fire, and other local, State, and Federal participants in the regional emergency management sphere;

- How well the business continuity and security plans are informed by regional partners in the Communications, Information Technology, Transportation, and Energy sectors; and

- The development of information-sharing relationships with other financial institutions within each region.

The precursor of the first regional partnership was the SIA Business Continuity Committee formed in December 2001. This committee was an outgrowth of the New York-based coalition of large financial services firms known as SIBCMG (Securities Industry Business Continuity Management Group). The informal relationships established by this committee have enhanced the resilience of these firms and the Nation's securities markets.

More formal initiatives in other regions have followed the efforts in New York. For example, in 2003, ChicagoFIRST became the first formal regional partnership within the financial sector, and it has since been followed by numerous others. The composition of these organizations varies from the various financial charters within ChicagoFIRST and FloridaFIRST to the combination of financial and non-financial members of partnerships in Minneapolis and San Francisco.

The Treasury, the FBIIC, and the FSSCC have encouraged and supported regional partnerships. To aid this process, the Treasury, ChicagoFIRST and BITS, a FSSCC member, created a "cookbook" guide for establishing regional coalitions, *Improving Business*

Continuity in the Financial Services Sector: A Model for Starting Regional Coalitions.[14] In addition, Congress promoted the establishment of regional partnerships within the financial sector in the Intelligence Reform and Terrorism Prevention Act of 2004.[15]

Following the success of ChicagoFIRST and the subsequent promotion of the regional partnership concept, regional partnerships have formed in many areas of the country, including the following:

Figure 1-3: Regional Partnerships

| Regional Partnerships |
|---|
| Chicago  (ChicagoFIRST) |
| Miami  (FloridaFIRST) |
| Tampa  (FloridaFIRST) |
| San Francisco  (Bay Area Response Coalition (BARC FIRST)) |
| Los Angeles  (SoCalFIRST) |
| Minneapolis  (MN-ISAC and Minnesota Security Board) |
| Birmingham  (Alabama Recovery Coalition for the Financial Sector) |
| Houston  (HoustonFIRST) |

In addition to these formally established partnerships, several other regions in the United States are aggressively pursuing the formation of such organizations in their region or State.

In 2006, in order to share best practices, assist one another, and plug into the existing national public/private partnership, these regional partnerships formed the Regional Partnership Council, called RPC FIRST. The organization meets quarterly and is developing a Web site.

[14] www.treas.gov/press/releases/reports/chicagofirst_handbook.pdf.
[15] www.gpoaccess.gov/serialset/creports/intel_reform.html.

Figure 1-4: Locations of Regional Partnerships

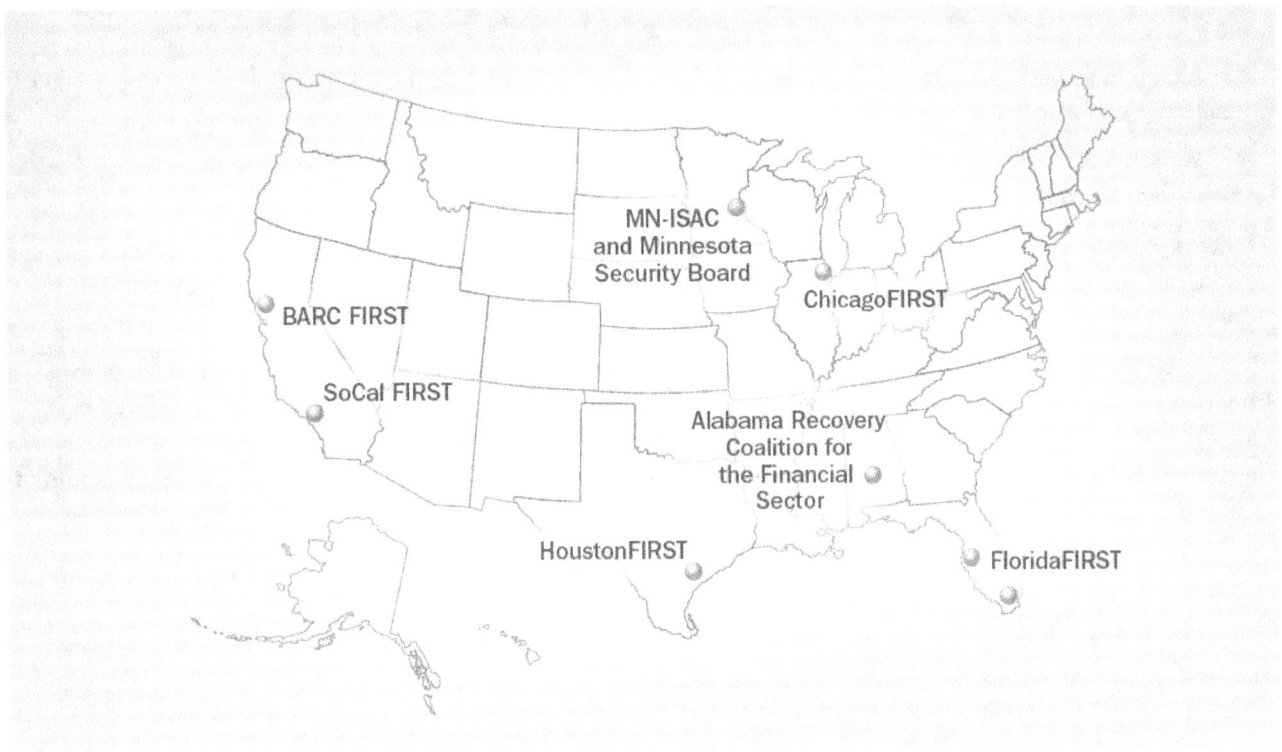

## 1.3 Sector Security Goals

The Banking and Finance Sector is strong and resilient, with an infrastructure that is designed to respond quickly and appropriately to detect, deter, prevent, and mitigate physical and cyber-based intrusions, attacks, or other emergencies. This ability ensures the continuity and efficient operation of the sector's institutions, and thereby serves to strengthen public confidence in the U.S. economic system.

---

### Vision Statement for the Banking and Finance Sector

*To continue to improve the resilience and availability of financial services, the Banking and Finance Sector will work through its public-private partnership to address the evolving nature of threats and the risks posed by the sector's dependency upon other critical sectors.*

---

The Banking and Finance Sector has three primary goals to achieve this vision statement. As with all endeavors focused primarily on security, the goals form a triad of prevention, detection, and correction of harm with the following objectives for the sector:

1. To maintain its strong position of resilience, risk management, and redundant systems, in the face of a myriad of intentional, unintentional, manmade, and natural threats;

2. To address and manage the risks posed by the dependence of the sector on the Communications, Information Technology, Energy, and Transportation sectors; and

3. To work with the law enforcement community, the private sector, and our international counterparts to increase the amount of available resources dedicated to tracking and catching criminals responsible for crimes against the sector, including cyber attacks and other electronic crimes.

The agencies are mindful of the risk that an unanticipated event, such as a terrorist attack, could occur in a manner that we have not seen before and for which we may not be completely prepared. Moreover, we live with the continuing threat of turbulent weather, which could severely damage the critical infrastructure and facilities of financial services firms. In addition, the financial services industry cannot fully protect against infrastructure disruptions of telecommunications, and it can provide only limited resilience against disruptions in other elements of the critical infrastructure, such as power, transportation, and water.[16]

## 1.4 Value Proposition

The public and private sectors have equally compelling value propositions to support their voluntary participation in sector-wide resilience efforts, including this SSP.

For financial regulators, working collaboratively with the private sector furthers the important mission to promote the orderly and efficient operation of the financial services sector. While financial regulators enforce extensive regulation and conduct regular examinations of the institutions, voluntary collaboration with the private sector has proved to be an effective method to garner industry-wide participation in the identification of emerging and dynamic risks and preparation of response capabilities. Through information sharing, testing, and exercises, regulators are able to better understand sector-wide vulnerabilities and resilience. These efforts provide a means for addressing dynamic risks through voluntary collaboration rather than solely through regulation.

For private sector institutions and organizations, participation in voluntary collaborative efforts provides value in several ways. Working alongside the public sector provides unique insights into regulators' concerns, perspectives, and priorities. Through relationship building, information sharing, testing, and exercises, financial institutions are able to discuss matters outside of the normal regulatory framework. Most importantly, financial institutions and financial services organizations participate in these voluntary efforts because of the concrete value they provide to their companies and, in turn, their customers. Customers must have confidence in their financial institution's ability to maintain orderly operations and to be highly resilient. Participating in these voluntary sector-wide efforts provides institutions with a better understanding of vulnerabilities within the sector as well as risks posed by its dependence on other sectors. Insights gained through voluntary collaboration assist financial institutions' efforts to tailor responses to manage their specific risk as well as sector-wide risk. In turn, the financial institutions are better able to meet their customers' demand for a high degree of resilience and reliability.

---

[16] www.federalreserve.gov/boarddocs/rptcongress/soundpractices/soundpractices200604.pdf.

# 2. Identify Assets, Systems, Networks, and Functions

Essential to conducting a risk assessment of the Banking and Finance Sector is the awareness that the products of the financial services industry are not overwhelmingly physical in nature. Thus, identifying and assessing assets in the sector is focused largely on identifying critical processes based on the organization of the sector as described in chapter 1, and the institutions that either own and operate or participate in these processes, rather than focusing on physical assets.

Figure 2.1: Vulnerability Assessment Methodology

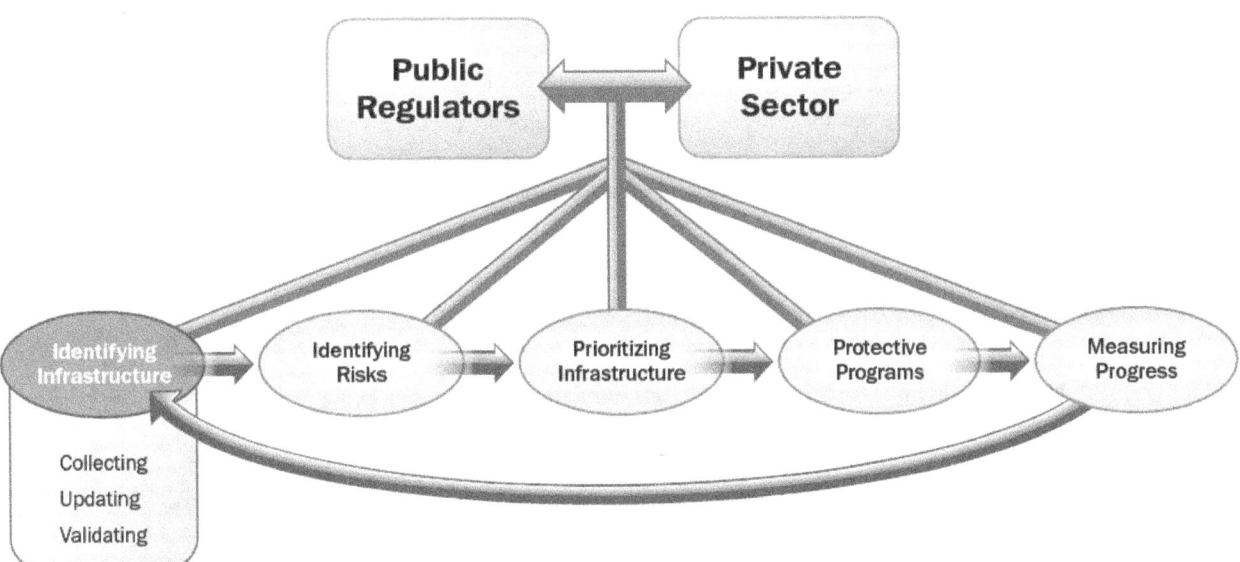

Many institutions play important roles in the financial system. Identifying institutions that have systemically critical operational roles is relevant to make certain of their rapid recovery from a disruption of their critical functions, regardless of the cause. Identifying those institutions also is necessary for imposing appropriate business continuity planning and recovery standards and ensuring their compliance with those standards. After careful consideration, the Treasury Department and the FBIIC agencies have identified a small number of systemically critical institutions whose operations form the backbone of the financial system. All of the systemically critical institutions are subject to some form of Government oversight, and their resilience is a matter of keen interest. As technology and innovation advance the operations of financial services firms, the list of systemically critical institutions may evolve over time.

There are also institutions or groups of institutions that, while not systemically critical, play significant roles in critical financial markets. Consequences of disruption at these organizations would vary. For example, an operational disruption at the largest banks and firms with significant payment or market activities could be tolerated for a limited time, while disruptions at others may be tolerated for longer periods, especially if their operations could be shifted or performed by other market participants. After September 11, 2001, the securities markets and several futures exchanges were closed until telecommunications and other services were restored to lower Manhattan. The fact that these markets and new transactions were affected for a short period of time did not result in significant damage to or loss of confidence in the U.S. financial system.

Diversity within the financial services sector and geographic dispersion of its institutions lend significant resilience to the Banking and Finance Sector. In addition to the systemically critical institutions described above, the U.S. financial system consists of many thousands of depository institutions, securities and futures firms, insurance companies, and other financial service companies, and supports a number of exchanges and over-the-counter markets, all of which provide a high degree of redundancy across the sector. The competitive structure of the financial industry and the breadth of the financial instruments provide a level of resiliency against attack and other types of physical or cyber disruptions. Accordingly, for purposes of determining systemic vulnerabilities, these institutions, while certainly important to the financial system, are not considered systemically critical.

## 2.1 Defining Information Parameters

The Banking and Finance Sector may be divided into several functions: deposit and payments systems; credit and liquidity products; investment products; and risk transfer products. Various members of the FBIIC regulate each of these functions as outlined in section 1.1. The financial regulators, through their oversight authority, obtain a vast amount of information on institutions, critical assets and processes, and potential vulnerabilities. Sector-wide risks assessments are process-driven and address interdependence. Individual institutions also conduct their own risk assessments to identify and mitigate internal vulnerabilities and external dependencies.

The Treasury Department, through collaboration and insights obtained from the members of the FBIIC and the FSSCC, gathers sector-specific information. Although the definition of asset data is limited to the categories collected by the regulators, regulatory examinations and trade association surveys are thorough and provide adequate information for defining financial assets.

General information for assets may include as appropriate to each component of the sector:

- Asset name, mailing address, physical location, owner/operator name;
- Function or type of transaction: deposit and payments systems; credit and liquidity products, including investment and risk transfer;
- Geographic region, financial center;
- Number of employees;
- Economic contribution: total market value of financial transactions conducted by or through the asset on a daily, weekly, monthly, and yearly basis;
- International considerations, if any;
- Existing and planned protective measures;

- Membership in a regional partnership or ISAC;

- Dependence on other sectors: Communications, Energy, Information Technology, and Transportation;

- Interaction with other assets: those other critical national assets directly and indirectly affected by the operation of each asset;

- Backup capability: location and function of backup facilities (data center and business resumption); and

- Substitutability: whether other industry systems or infrastructures would be able to serve the same function.

Intangible assets, such as systems, databases, or networks, are in one way or another linked to physical assets and locations. Systemically significant assets are stratified by their examination agency with respect to criticality to the financial services sector as a whole.

## 2.2 Collecting Infrastructure Information

The Treasury Department's and the Federal and State financial regulators' expertise in the financial services sector has been shaped by 217 years of experience. Continuous financial regulatory examinations and reporting requirements provide the financial regulatory agencies with voluminous and consistently updated data on institutions' operations and finances. Through the collaborative efforts of the FBIIC, the financial regulatory authorities have assessed the Banking and Finance Sector, identifying strengths and weaknesses within the domestic financial system, as well as pinpointing some institutions that play a systemically critical role within the sector.

In the private sector, financial trade associations regularly collect and share information on their member institutions for policy development. For example, the FSSCC members surveyed their members on lessons learned from the Northeast Blackout of 2003 and Hurricane Katrina in 2005. This effort helps to guide policymakers in understanding the needs of the sector in preparation for future events. The FSSCC members also gathered information on the participation of their members in programs such as Government Emergency Telecommunications Service (GETS), Wireless Priority Service (WPS), and Telecommunications Service Priority (TSP). This information helps to target those organizations that qualify for these services but are not yet taking advantage of them.

### 2.2.1 Deposit and Payment System Products

The depository institution system is supported by electronic payment systems that link these institutions to one another and to their customers. Examples of these systems and networks are the many regional/national ATM networks[17] that permit consumers to access their funds from more than 1.5 million ATM sites worldwide;[18] four major credit card sponsors;[19] and the ACH operators, which processed nearly 14 billion payments worth more than $27.9 trillion in 2005.[20] Businesses and consumers increasingly use ACH payment systems to make recurring payments (e.g., creditor withdrawal of the customers' monthly mortgage and other recurring payments).[21]

Several other payment systems, such as the Clearing House Interbank Payments System (CHIPS) and Fedwire, support larger value payments. In 2005, the Fedwire payments systems sent 132 million payments, valued at $518 trillion per year over its system, with an average transaction size of $3.9 million. During the same period, the CHIPS payment network sent 71 million payments valued at $350 trillion with an average size of $4.9 million per payment. It is important to note that these systems may be

[17] ATM networks generally support both ATM and Personal Identification Number (PIN)-based debit card transactions.

[18] ATM Industry Association Europe.

[19] These merchants have 55 million locations (merchants and ATMs) worldwide. The four major credit card companies are Visa, MasterCard, American Express, and Discover.

[20] www.nacha.org/News/news/pressreleases/2006/Pr050806/pr050806.htm.

[21] By comparison, $2.3 trillion worth of payments and another $1.2 trillion worth of securities settlements typically are made daily through the Federal Reserve's large-value payment system, while another $1.7 trillion are made over CHIPS, also a large-value system.

linked to payments occurring in systems outside the United States. Also, the securities clearing systems such as the Depository Trust & Clearing Corporation (DTCC) for the equities and government securities markets and The Options Clearing Corporation for the securities derivatives markets, process more than 8.35 billion transactions worth $1.01 quadrillion annually.[22]

Retail customers are increasingly processing their transactions with their depository institutions via the Internet. Financial regulators have issued extensive guidance to these institutions on how to manage this activity and mitigate the risks associated.

These deposit and payment system products are governed by a complex system of requirements, generally promulgated by Federal banking agencies, the SEC, or private SROs or rule-making bodies. The organizations operating payment systems are examined for compliance purposes by the appropriate agencies. For example, distinct Federal regulations govern the processing of funds stemming from checks, and inter-bank funds transfers, while ACH payments are governed by rules promulgated by NACHA-The Electronics Payment Association.

### 2.2.2 Credit and Liquidity Products

Credit markets are not formal markets with either a physical location or one narrow set of methods that define them. Rather, there are a wide variety of financial firms that provide credit and financing, including more than 17,000 depository institutions in the United States,[23] and a wide variety of non-depository providers, including mortgage financing firms, and many others. Moreover, many of the financial firms that provide financing at retail institutions require liquidity to fund their financing activity.

The number of financial services providers of credit and liquidity is extremely large, due to the many specialized niche markets serviced and the often highly tailored financial services provided. Given the many types of products, there is no single set of systems at work that dominates these financial products. However, throughout the entire financial services sector there are rigid goals of safeguarding the assets of clients and ensuring that client assets, the financial firms' assets, and recordkeeping systems are highly resilient to any foreseeable event.

### 2.2.3 Investment Products

Collectively, the thousands of investment service providers own more than $16 trillion[24] in financial assets. Many of these providers operate in a highly regulated environment governed by a complex legal structure.

Some of these investment products are provided on highly formalized financial markets, while others are provided by regulated financial services providers not acting specifically in a formal financial market. Examples of highly developed formal financial markets include financial exchanges, at which financial assets are traded in a tightly regulated manner so as to achieve the desired purposes of market participants.

These formal financial markets have highly developed and extremely efficient, redundant networks and systems that provide a high degree of resilience for these markets in the face of a variety of potential situations. Additionally, these networks incorporate strong safeguards to protect clients' assets and provide both the customers and institutions with consistent access to their funds and records.

### 2.2.4 Risk-Transfer Products

Risk-transfer products include insurance and hedging instruments such as futures and options. Hedging instruments valued at close to $1 quadrillion are traded annually.[25] Insurance covers in excess of $6 trillion[26] worth of assets. Financial risk-transfer

---

[22] www.dtcc.com/AboutUs/2005annual/dtcc2005_annual.pdf and www.theocc.com/about/ann_rep/ann_rep_pdf/annual_rep_05.pdf.

[23] www2.fdic.gov/sod/sodSumReport.asp?barItem=3&sInfoAsOf=2006 and www.ncua.gov/data/FOIA/foia.html.

[24] www.federalreserve.gov/releases/Z1/Current/annuals/a1995-2005.pdf.

[25] www.cme.com/about/ins/caag/FacFigu2803.html and www.theocc.com/about/ann_rep/ann_rep_pdf/annual_rep_05.pdf.

[26] www.federalreserve.gov/releases/Z1/Current/annuals/a1995-2005.pdf.

products often are tailored to the unique nature of the risks involved, although there are numerous standardized financial risk-transfer products, such as those traded on options and futures exchanges. Thus, the networks and systems used by the institutions providing these services often are tailored to the individual financial firm.

### 2.2.5 Collecting Asset Data

To meet the challenge of more complex financial markets, products, and delivery systems, financial institutions—in particular, large financial institutions—have been implementing more formal and complex risk management systems. Similarly, the regulators have refined their approach to supervision of financial institutions of all sizes by adopting a risk-focused approach to meet new challenges. Some regulators assign a staff of full-time examiners, who work on site, to the largest, most complex financial institutions. This on-site presence allows regulators to receive updated information about larger firms on a daily basis. Federal, and at times State, law gives financial regulatory agencies broad authority to access records held or maintained by regulated financial institutions.[27] That information generally is provided exclusively to the financial regulatory agency, although in the event of potential criminal law violations, mechanisms exist to share that information with law enforcement agencies, including those within DHS.

The Treasury Department will continue to collect data on critical assets by coordinating with the FBIIC agencies.

## 2.3 Verifying Infrastructure Information

The Treasury Department, through the members of the FBIIC, uses a three-part process to verify asset information. First, a drafting committee collects and verifies the information. Second, the FBIIC members review the information for accuracy and errors. Third, a special FBIIC review committee subjects each asset assessment to rigorous questioning and review.

## 2.4 Updating Infrastructure Information

The information gathered through the examination process provides access to infrastructure information on the Banking and Finance Sector. The Treasury Department, through the members of the FBIIC, updates asset data on an as-needed basis.

The frequent examinations processes undertaken by the financial regulatory agencies ensure that up-to-date information is maintained regarding all facets of the regulated financial institutions, and the financial services industry regularly updates its regulators regarding both highly significant as well as routine changes.

---

[27] Some of those sources of Federal statutory authority are contained in Titles 12 and 15 of the United States Code. (See appendix 2 for details.)

# 3. Assess Risks

Both the public and private members of the Banking and Finance Sector conduct risk assessments. These assessments look at issues and potential vulnerabilities both within individual organizations and sector-wide. Since risk management is part of the banking and finance culture, both regulators and private organization have a long history of conducting regular risk assessments. In the private sector some of these risk assessments are mandated through regulation and validated by the examination process. Furthermore, the private sector institutions conduct voluntary risk assessments to meet their business needs as part of their continuity panning and/or in conjunction with trade associations' recommendations and self-regulatory requirements.

Following the attacks of September 11, 2001, the sector's risk assessment efforts became more formalized and took on a renewed sense of urgency. The FBIIC began an organized annual effort to examine the financial sector's resilience. The process has continued and matured over the years to include physical and cyber-based components of the sector as well as dependencies on other critical sectors. Information in this process is garnered through the regulators' extensive knowledge of sector participants. Furthermore, this information is verified through consultation with key private sector organizations. Information shared between the members of the sector and the financial regulators provide insights into the operational, financial, and systemic risks facing individual organizations and the sector as a whole. Through organizations such as the Federal Financial Institutions Examinations Council (FFIEC), various private sector trade associations, and the FBIIC, there is ongoing verification and validation updating of risk assessment information. Furthermore, through individual information-sharing efforts between the Treasury Department and individual financial institutions, this process is furthered informed regarding new and emerging threats.

Through this process, the Treasury Department has identified potential limitations and created a process to identify and assess vulnerabilities within the sector.

The following sections refer to the efforts of the Treasury Department, working with the FBIIC members and the private sector, to identify sector vulnerabilities and assess the risks across the Banking and Finance Sector.

Figure 3-1: Vulnerability Assessment Methodology

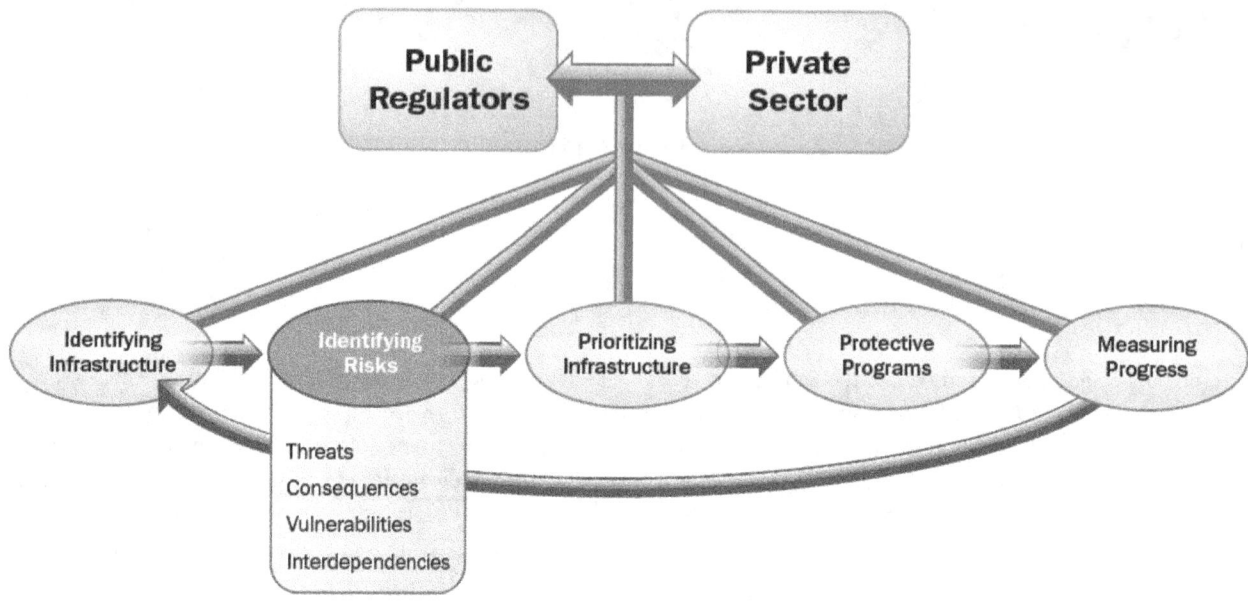

## 3.1 Use of Risk Assessment in the Sector

The Banking and Finance Sector has a long-standing and accepted practice of conducting risk assessments and mitigating vulnerabilities. These risk assessments take into account NIPP baseline assessment criteria, including consequences, vulnerabilities, and threats to the essential underlying clearing, payment, and settlements systems of the sector. These assessments also consider vulnerabilities stemming from direct or indirect threats to the physical and cyber-based operations across the sector. Furthermore, these assessments consider the nature of the incident, be it natural or manmade. The focus of these sector-wide assessments is on the potential impact that such risks, if exploited, would have on the orderly and efficient operation of the sector.

In the private sector, consequence analysis assessment methodology includes potential economic impacts to the institution, reputation risk to the institution, and potential impacts to the employees and surrounding population and facilities depending on the nature of the incident.

In the public sector, each regulatory agency examines the individual entities within their purview based upon a risk management framework. This regimen has been fine-tuned over an extended period of time to address risk as it pertains to the resilience and integrity of both the individual institutions and the financial system as a whole. Consequence analysis in risk assessment methodologies in the public sector include potential economic impact, impact on public confidence in the financial system, and impact to the Government's ability to continue to provide its services to the public. These methodologies are complete, accurate, and reproducible in accordance with the NIPP baseline criteria. The assessments are updated daily through the intense and extensive regulatory examination process.

Collectively, the public sector, under the auspices of the FBIIC, carefully analyzes the entire U.S. financial system to assess its strength and resilience to manmade and natural disasters. Relying upon their collective expertise and experience, the members of the FBIIC developed a specialized risk assessment methodology for the Banking and Finance Sector. Based on this methodology, the FBIIC agencies identify financial institutions that play significant roles in key financial markets either individually or as a group. The vulnerabilities assessments address physical and cyber weaknesses in the financial services sector and are representative of both kinds of incidents. Collectively, these risk assessments provide an overall risk profile of the sector.

## 3.2 Screening Infrastructure

As stated in section 1, the Banking and Finance Sector may be divided into several functions: deposit and payments systems; credit and liquidity products; investment products; and risk-transfer products. The Treasury Department and members of the FBIIC use a screening process to identify certain assets within the Banking and Finance Sector that are systemically important.

The sector is constantly changing, as are the dynamic screening efforts of the FBIIC to identify these systemically important assets. The Treasury Department and the FBIIC continually meet with financial institutions and regulators to determine any new assets that are critical to the operations of the sector. When a new asset is identified, the Treasury and the FBIIC take appropriate actions to address any vulnerability related to that asset.

The described asset data are controlled by the Treasury Department and the members of the FBIIC. The Treasury and key stakeholders in the public and private sectors update the asset data on an as-needed basis.

## 3.3 Assessing Consequences

The Banking and Finance Sector assesses the consequences of an asset's loss or impairment within the context of its impact on the sector's ability to operate efficiently and in an orderly manner and its potential impact on the public's confidence in the financial system as a whole. Several factors used in this assessment include diversity, redundancy, nature of dependence on the asset, network or system, and symbolic importance.

## 3.4 Assessing Vulnerabilities

The Banking and Finance Sector conducts ongoing vulnerability assessments. These vulnerability assessments include examinations into the potential risks resulting from cross-sector dependency, sector-specific vulnerabilities and dependencies on key assets, systems, technologies, and processes. These assessments are based upon the extensive knowledge of regulators and guidance issued, and take into account physical, cyber, and human vulnerabilities, available redundancy, and the sector's reliance on sector-specific assets, systems and processes, and cross-sector reliance on these factors. Consequence assessments include direct economic impacts and national confidence impacts, and are based on expert judgment and exercises.

Through the vulnerability assessments, the sector has determined that some of its greatest challenges are its dependence on the telecommunications network and the power grid. Also, the Treasury Department and the FBIIC have identified the following additional important sector dependencies: Communications, Energy, Information Technology, and Transportation systems. As addressed in chapter 5 on protective programs, various efforts are underway to address these dependence risks.

Figure 3-2: Dependent Relationships

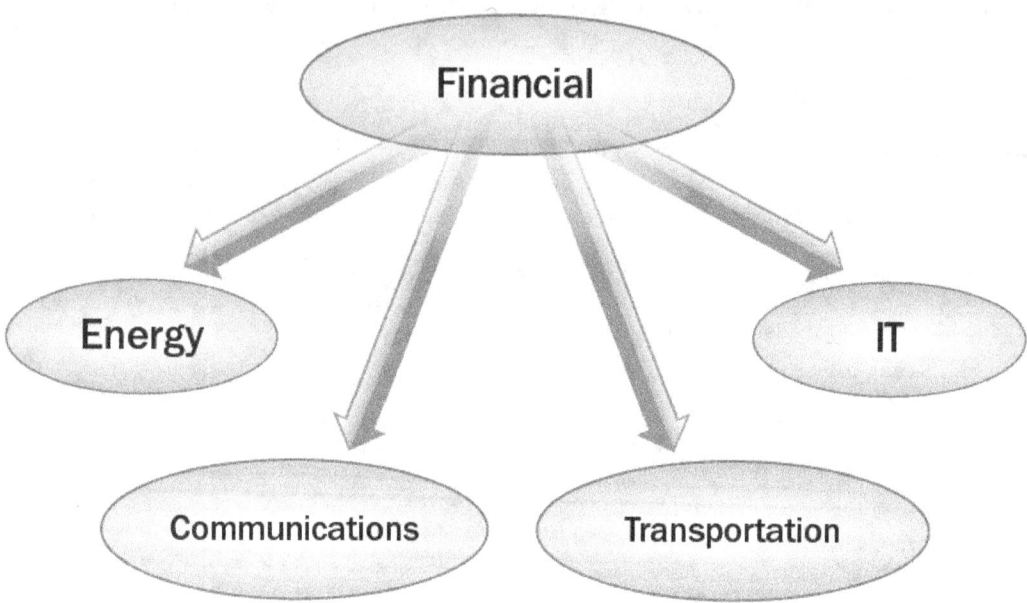

Any vulnerability assessment of the financial services sector cannot be truly final because the sector is evolving constantly. Thus, the FBIIC members continue to update assessments regularly to identify vulnerabilities and manage and assess asset risks, especially as the sector adopts new technology. Furthermore, the Treasury Department will work with DHS to coordinate how to normalize the results of the Banking and Finance Sector's vulnerability assessments so that they may be comparable to the overall NIPP.

## 3.5 Assessing Threats

There have been individuals and groups that have attempted to exploit the sector for their own pecuniary gains. Over time, the sector has developed defenses to thwart these attacks. However, criminals and terrorists continue to devise new methods and schemes. Therefore, the Treasury works with other Federal agencies, including the DHS Homeland Infrastructure Threat and Risk Analysis Center (HITRAC), on a daily basis to assess physical and cyber threats that are identified as specifically directed at the sector or at an asset on a national, regional, or local level. Relationships with DHS and other SSAs provide real-time information regarding these threats. Additionally, when threats are identified, frequent communications between the FBIIC and the FSSCC facilitate the efficient and effective transfer of potential threat information, permitting the sector to mitigate vulnerabilities.

# 4. Prioritize Infrastructure

In the wake of the attacks of September 11, 2001, the Treasury, in conjunction with the members of the FBIIC and the private sector, undertook a renewed effort to identify and prioritize the key infrastructures. This effort is part of the overall risk assessment and management process taking place in the public and private sectors on an ongoing basis. The risk assessment methodology discussed in section 3 is part of the sector's overall risk management approach, which includes prioritization efforts. The prioritization within this approach assists the sector in determining the focus for protective programs.

In the private sector, this effort is an internal process to analyze and prioritize the processes and networks that the individual institutions need to meet their business continuity management and planning efforts.

In the public sector, the Treasury Department, through outreach to the members of the FBIIC, conducts an annual risk assessment review of the sector. This effort provides a sector-wide prioritization focused on business continuity and resilience for essential processes in the Banking and Finance Sector. The prioritization is informed by the extensive knowledge of the members of the FBIIC and, where appropriate, in consultation with certain private sector owners and operators. As the sector is changing constantly, so, too, are the Treasury and the FBIIC's processes for identifying and prioritizing the systemically important assets, processes, and networks. The Treasury Department and the FBIIC continually meet with financial institutions and regulators to determine any new assets that are critical to the operations of the sector. Results from these consultations are used to update the annual prioritization where appropriate.

The Treasury Department uses the prioritization to inform sector participants where appropriate and to facilitate discussions, if necessary, to employ protective measures with the owners and operators. In specific instances, the Treasury Department reaches out to these members of the sector to encourage participation in business continuity exercises and programs. From a sector-wide perspective, these prioritization efforts inform the FBIIC's perspective on overall sector risk and, in turn, influence the Treasury Department's ongoing development of new outreach programs.

Furthermore the Treasury Department works with its security partners, including DHS, to collaborate on threat analysis and information dissemination in accordance with this prioritization in the Banking and Finance Sector. This process enables the coordination necessary to conform with the NIPP baseline criteria and helps to facilitate DHS's efforts to assess national comparable risk.

The basis for prioritization of critical infrastructure within the Banking and Finance Sector stems from the degree of sector reliance on the identified assets, processes, and networks. Analysis for this prioritization relies upon the potential impact to the sector's continued efficient and orderly operation, should the infrastructure experience significant interruption or loss. Essential to this prioritization process is the importance of these infrastructures and the overall financial services system to maintaining the public's confidence in our national economic system and political institutions. The effort uses a variety of factors, including:

- The degree of industry dependence on the asset;

- The presence or absence of alternative suppliers of the services performed by the asset;

- The public need for the services provided by the asset;

- The potential impact of a disruption on the asset to the financial system;

- The potential impacts on the economy through the cascading disruption of other CI/KR; and

- Trends and specific information in threat analysis.

Figure 4-1: Vulnerability Assessment Methodology

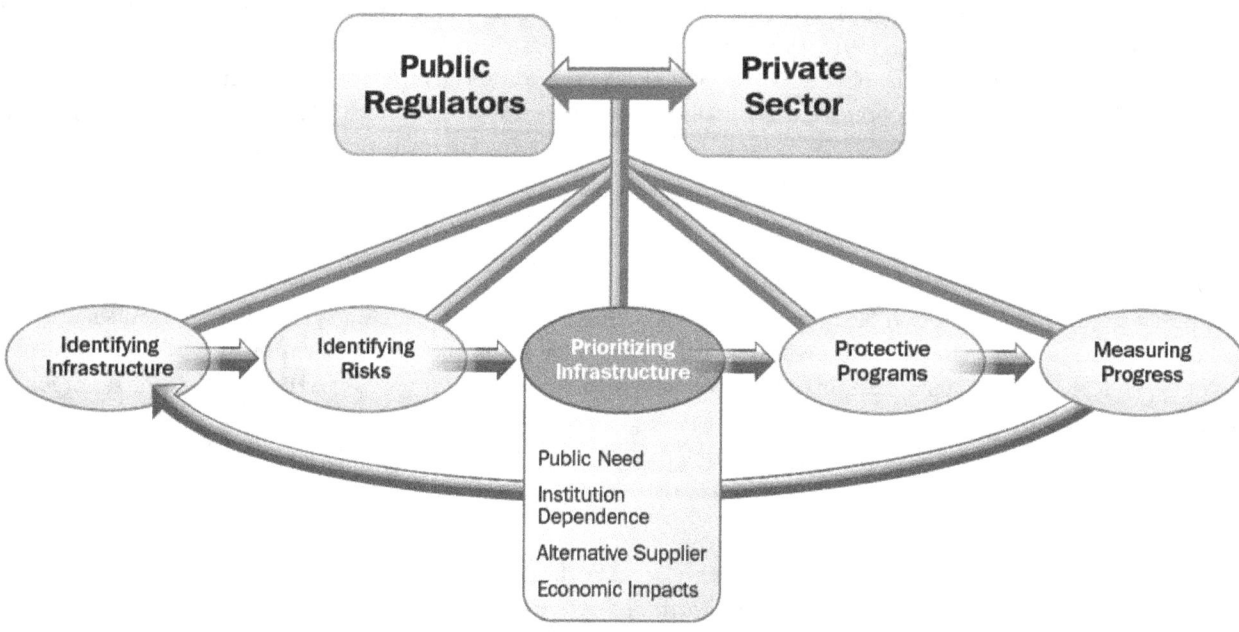

# 5. Develop and Implement Protective Programs

## 5.1 Overview of Sector Protective Programs

Due to the highly diverse and decentralized nature of the Banking and Finance Sector, and the fact that the sector is largely owned and operated by the private sector, public and private sector owners and operators must share responsibility for ensuring the orderly and efficient operation of the sector and meeting the sector's security goals.

Figure 5-1: Vulnerability Assessment Methodology

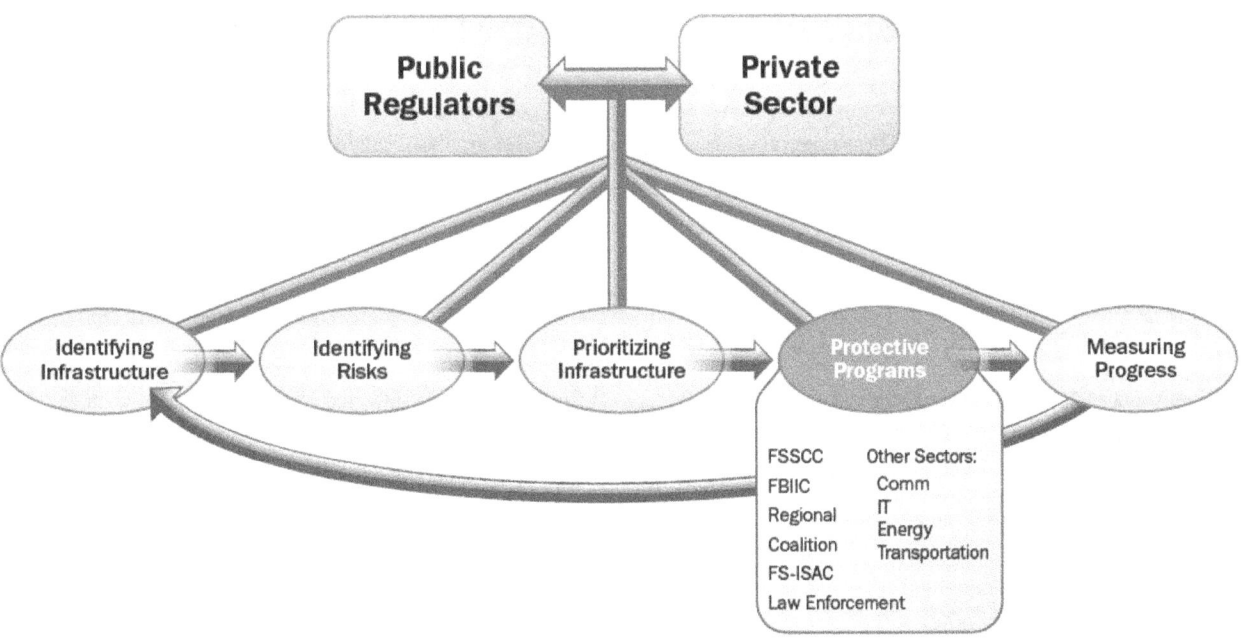

## 5.2 Determining Protective Program Needs

Through direct mandated and regulatory authority, the public sector plays an essential role in the development of private sector protective programs. For example, during the events of September 11, 2001, the FRB, in its role as the central bank, sought to provide sufficient liquidity to the markets by lending through the discount window, buying Treasury securities through open market operations, and entering into currency swaps with other central banks. These tools may be used in efforts to maintain the stability of the financial system and contain systemic risks that may arise in financial markets. Furthermore, the strong public-private partnerships outlined in this section have facilitated the development of a collaborative and voluntary process to develop protective programs. These programs are based on the results of the sector's vulnerability assessment and the extensive knowledge of the financial regulators and private sector participants. Additionally, the sector conducts numerous exercises that help to underscore areas that may need updating of existing programs or new collaborative efforts.

## 5.3 Protective Program Implementation

The Treasury Department, the FBIIC, and the FSSCC have a number of protective program initiatives in progress or completed to address the security goals outlined in chapter 2.

Goal 1: To maintain its current strong position of resilience, risk management, and redundant systems in the face of a myriad of intentional, unintentional, manmade, and natural threats, the Banking and Finance Sector has undertaken and continues to develop and/or conduct the following protective programs:

- The FBIIC is a robust, formal information-sharing organization for the financial regulatory community, which includes cross subsector representation, Federal authorities, and State regulatory authority trade associations;

  - The FBIIC meets quarterly to discuss progress on research, exercises, protective measures, and emerging risks, and to identify new means for continuing progress toward improving the resilience of the sector.

  - The FBIIC and the FSSCC sponsor outreach meetings throughout the country entitled "Protecting the Financial Sector, a Public and Private Partnership." These meetings inform financial institutions about the many public and private programs that enhance homeland security.

- The FSSCC is a robust, formal private sector organization that shares information, promotes best practices, and identifies sector priorities;

  - The FSSCC meets quarterly to discuss progress on research, exercises, protective measures, and emerging risks, and to identify new means for continuing progress toward improving the resilience of the sector.

  - The FSSCC and its member organizations reported on recent efforts in support of this goal in the FSSCC document, *Protecting the U.S. Critical Financial Infrastructure: 2005 in Review*. This report is available on the FSSCC's Web site as is the FSSCC's Annual Report for 2004.[28]

- Strong emergency management communication protocols facilitate information sharing during a crisis, with quarterly testing of our protocols;

- Coordination with foreign regulatory agencies, such as the U.K. Financial Services Authority with respect to exercises and testing, improves the emergency preparedness of critical financial institutions;

- The FS-ISAC is a formal organization that dispenses specific threat- and vulnerability-related information daily, including physical and cyber, largely to the private sector;

---

[28] www.fsscc.org/publications.

- The Treasury Department acquired $2 million in services from the FS-ISAC which had the added benefit of creating the next generation FS-ISAC by increasing the protective functions of sharing and distributing information among the FS-ISAC members, and improving the tracking and measurement of the FS-ISAC's performance.

- The FS-ISAC has provided the following deliverables on behalf of the sector:

  - Worked closely with the other ISACs in the development of a Framework for Operational Information/Intelligence Sharing Between the ISACs. The purpose of this framework is to provide a useful operational guide for encouraging broad participation in information sharing among and between all public-private critical infrastructure sectors;

  - Implemented a crisis communications system to notify all of its members within less than 1 hour of an emergency. This system has been modified to include a subgroup of all the FSSCC members;

  - Developed a searchable database of past and current incidents, vulnerabilities, and threat data, along with an extensive e-library of important security and infrastructure protection documents; and

  - Developed threat vulnerability and incident management best practices.

- Regional partnerships share information pertinent on a local level to address specific local needs and establish relationships on a local level with key decisionmakers. The number of these regional partnerships continues to expand and have provided the following activities:

  - Coordinate the Federal and State response to regional financial sector crises. One example includes partnering with ChicagoFIRST and the Chicago Office of Emergency Management and Communications.

  - Developed a handbook based on the ChicagoFIRST model to foster regional associations of financial services firms that address CIP issues at the State, local, and tribal levels.

  - Formed and continue to grow a council of regional partnerships, called RPC FIRST, to foster collaboration, share best practices, and coordinate with the FSSCC and the FBIIC.

  - Conduct exercises with local emergency management officials and State and Federal officials on areas of threat to the region.

- Protective response planning exercises with the Treasury Department and several private sector financial institutions focus on an explicit threat to a systemically critical financial institution. These exercises provide financial institutions and local law enforcement with a protective response plan, through joint programs that include first responders;

- Information from various cyber protection alert services is shared and disseminated through established communication protocols;

- Collaborative relationships with law enforcement and intelligence communities to monitor new and emerging threats and to mitigate those threats and vulnerabilities;

- A research agenda addresses sector-specific goals. (See section 7 for details);

- A joint initiative with the National Infrastructure Advisory Council (NIAC) on the Pandemic Prioritization Initiative to ensure that critical financial services functions continue in the event of pandemic influenza; and

- Regular meetings of the Infectious Disease Forum. This Forum, which was established by the FSSCC and is led by the Securities Industry and Financial Markets Association (SIFMA), provides a venue for the FSSCC members to collaborate among themselves and with members of the FBIIC and with other sectors upon which the Banking and Finance Sector is dependent.

Goal 2: To address and manage the risks posed by the dependence of the sector on the Communications, Information Technology, Energy, and Transportation sectors, the financial regulators and private sector are performing the following:

- Conducting research with other Federal partners on the financial sector's reliance on telecommunications infrastructure;

- Working with other critical infrastructure sectors and appropriate Government agencies to address critical interdependencies including telecommunications diversity and resilience and electrical power grid vulnerabilities;

- Sponsoring private sector firms that qualify under the National Security and Emergency Preparedness guidelines for GETS, WPS, and TSP. The GETS and WPS grant priority access over the telecommunications public network during emergencies. The TSP users receive priority restoration;

- Issuing guidance and conducting regular examinations of institutions' risk management of information technology, including system design, software design and management, hardware design and management, use of services and their service level agreements, and use of assurance products and services;

- Exclusively with respect to financial regulators, serving as members of the Government Coordinating Councils (GCC) for the Information Technology and Energy sectors;

- Working with Communications Sector participants to align the recovery timeframes for voice and data recovery capabilities so that they are consistent with the recovery measures established by the financial regulators for the Banking and Finance Sector.

- Working with Communications Sector participants to assess the vulnerability of the Communications Sector on which the Banking and Finance Sector is primarily dependent;

- Conducting research with academia and the private sector to develop a test bed for data flow and security;

- Developing a visualization modeling working group with the Department of Energy; and

- Meeting with and continuing to build relationships with representatives from the other sectors through the Partnership for Critical Infrastructure Security (PCIS) and presentations by other sectors at FSSCC meetings.

Goal 3: To advance the work of the law enforcement community, the private sector, and our international counterparts to increase the amount of available resources dedicated to tracking and catching criminals responsible for cyber attacks and other electronic crimes, the Treasury Department and members of the FBIIC are:

- Participating in DHS cyber-based exercises such as "Cyber Storm" and the NCRCG;

- Working with DHS to provide buffer zone protection plans for critical institutions; and

- Meeting with and supporting the efforts of Federal law enforcement, including the DOJ and the U.S. Secret Service.

### Going Forward

The resilience and strength of the financial services sector is dependent upon the collaboration and participation of the sector participants. The public-private partnership will help strengthen the resilience of the sector only if there is trust and cooperation between the public and private participants. Therefore, the Treasury Department will continue to coordinate with members of the FBIIC and the FSSCC to validate, update, and implement these metrics for the financial services sector, as necessary.

The Treasury Department, in the role of the SSA, and its public and private sector partners conduct and manage various implementation actions to achieve the Banking and Finance Sector's security goals. The following list is a compilation of the ongoing work of the SSA and various public and private sector participants, including the FBIIC agencies and the FSSCC members, as it relates to the sector metrics and security goals.

Goal 1: To maintain its current strong position of resilience, risk management, and redundant systems in the face of a myriad of intentional, unintentional, manmade, and natural threats, the Treasury Department, as the SSA, will work with the appropriate members of the FBIIC and the FSSCC to:

- Conduct at least three joint meetings per year of the FBIIC and the FSSCC;

- Conduct an appropriate number of joint meetings of working groups of the FBIIC and the FSSCC, such as the Infectious Disease Forum;

- Sponsor, organize, and encourage participation at outreach meetings to financial services representatives across the country regarding infrastructure protection issues, including how the FBIIC and the FSSCC operate as national partnerships and how regional coalitions are an important part of the national strategy;

- Sponsor private sector firms that qualify under the National Security and Emergency Preparedness guidelines for GETS, WPS, and TSP;

- Encourage the formation of new regional partnerships to share information pertinent on a local level, provide opportunities for institutions to address specific local needs, and establish relationships on a local level with key decisionmakers;

- Support RPC FIRST to foster collaboration, share best practices, and coordinate with the FSSCC and the FBIIC;

- Evaluate the percentage of assets that receive physical and cyber security alerts, either directly or indirectly through the FS-ISAC. The Treasury Department will consult with the FS-ISAC to determine the number of firms that receive physical and cyber security alerts either directly or through trade associations. Currently, there are 1,961 direct links from the FS-ISAC to financial institutions and an estimated 11,000 indirect links through member associations;

- Test the FS-ISAC's Critical Infrastructure Notification System (CINS) on a regular basis. As a matter of practice, the FSSCC members who are not members of FS-ISAC receive CINS notifications in the event of a FSSCC emergency;

- Work with DHS to appropriately coordinate the Homeland Security Information Network (HSIN) into the information-sharing structure for the sector;

- Participate in national and regional exercises to test and enhance the resilience of the financial services sector. For instance, the Banking and Finance Sector participated in Top Officials (TOPOFF) Exercise 3 and currently is assisting in the planning for TOPOFF Exercise 4. On a regional level, the Treasury Department has sponsored resilience exercises for ChicagoFIRST and FloridaFIRST and currently is working with other regional partnerships for future exercises;

- Conduct protective-response planning exercises for critical financial infrastructures. The Treasury Department, through the members of the FBIIC, will identify those firms that have participated in these types of exercises;

- Conduct briefings for the public and private stakeholders on the latest intelligence and threat assessments;

- Work with the sector participants to conduct tests to strengthen the response protocols for the FBIIC and the FSSCC;

- Encourage the financial services sector participants to develop, enhance, and test business continuity plans. Financial regulators have created and mandate stringent business recovery guidelines for their regulated institutions. In some cases the regulators, in their Interagency White Paper, have specified recovery timeframes for core clearing and settlement institutions (2 hours) and significant players (4 hours) in the event of a regional disaster;

- Support the FSSCC Research and Development (R&D) initiative, which is researching how to make financial services systems more resilient against cyber threats;

- Work with international organizations to look at issues related to financial management of large-scale disasters; and

- Conduct the appropriate review and update process by the Treasury Department and the FBIIC agencies for asset data on the sector.

**Goal 2: To address and manage the risks posed by the dependence of the sector on the Communications, Information Technology, Energy, and Transportation sectors, the Treasury Department, as the SSA, will work with the appropriate members of the FBIIC and the FSSCC to:**

- Invite participants from other sectors, including the Communications, Information Technology, Energy, and Transportation sectors, to the general and working group meetings of the FBIIC and the FSSCC to foster information sharing regarding cross-sector vulnerabilities and protective measures, and participate on the GCCs of other sectors, where permitted and appropriate;

- Work with the National Communications System (NCS) and other telecommunication partners to identify gaps;

- Work with the participants from the Communications, Information Technology, Energy, and Transportation sectors to determine the necessary level of redundancy and assurance to meet the vision statement of the Banking and Finance Sector;

- Participate in exercises modeling pandemics to pinpoint areas of concern where the financial services sector depends upon the infrastructure of other sectors; and

- Utilize the regional financial coalitions to coordinate discussions with State and local emergency managers and other sector partners.

**Goal 3: To advance the work of the law enforcement community, the private sector, and our international counterparts to increase the amount of available resources dedicated to tracking and catching criminals responsible for cyber attacks and other electronic crimes the Treasury Department, as the SSA, will work with the appropriate members of the FBIIC and the FSSCC to:**

- Orchestrate briefings between law enforcement, the financial services regulators, and the private sector when specified instances of cyber crime arise; and

- Assist with identifying and increasing awareness on emerging technologies that may assist with combating cyber crime or may be used by criminal elements to conduct cyber and other electronic crimes.

## 5.4 Protective Program Performance

As demonstrated in this section, the Treasury Department and members of the FBIIC, along with the private sector participants in the FSSCC and FS-ISAC, have developed many protective programs. These programs helped the Banking and Finance Sector endure the effects of September 11, 2001, as well as the major power outage in the northeastern United States (August 2003), and natural disasters, such as Hurricane Isabel (2003), Hurricane Katrina (2005), and Hurricane Rita (2005). Protective programs specific to pandemic planning also have been developed.

The following are some examples of protective program performance successes:

- In April 2003, the FRB, OCC, and SEC submitted to Congress the Financial System Resilience Report assessing the progress of core securities clearing and settlement organizations and significant securities firms in achieving the sound practices objectives articulated in the "Interagency White Paper";[29]

- In summer 2003, the FBIIC and the Treasury Department conducted a protective-response planning exercise with a systemically critical member of the sector;

---

[29] www.sec.gov/news/studies/34-47638.htm.

- In 2003, BITS and SIA drafted *Considerations for the Financial Services Industry: Actions Relevant to the Homeland Security Advisory System* on behalf of the FSSCC;

- In July 2004 when a credible threat was discovered which targeted financial services firms, the Treasury Department and the sector followed information-sharing and notification protocols. Furthermore, other firms in the vicinity of these targeted institutions employed internal protocols to increase protective measures in response to the heightened threat level;

- During 2004, the FSSCC produced suggested practices for sector members to use in protective programs, including pandemic planning;

- In 2004, the FBIIC and the FSSCC conducted its first phase of outreach meetings in 29 cities. At the end of the second phase in 2007, the outreach meetings will have reached 37 cities;

- In the first quarter of 2005, the Treasury Department, BITS, and ChicagoFIRST published a handbook on how to create regional organizations similar to ChicagoFIRST;

- In 2005 during Hurricane Katrina, the FS-ISAC provided reporting of the storm's predicted path well in advance of the hurricane hitting landfall. These reports included information on the potential impacts to transportation, telecommunications, water, health care, and financial services closings, as well as assistance strategies;

- In 2006, the FSSCC developed a Disaster Response Protocol for sharing information between the public and private sectors and rapid dissemination of information between organizations within the financial services sector;

- In 2006, the FS-ISAC developed and implemented threat advisory levels for both physical and cyber attacks to provide sector-specific threat warning to member institutions;

- During 2006, the Treasury Department and members of the FBIIC completed an updated vulnerability assessment of the sector;

- In November 2006, the Multi-State ISAC reported evidence of a brute-force cyber attack originating from Chinese IP source addresses. In response, the FS-ISAC shared member submissions with DHS and other ISACs, providing additional details and recommendations. As a result, the two IP source addresses were identified quickly and blocked;

- Throughout 2006, the FBIIC and the Treasury Department conducted two separate protective-response planning exercises with two different systemically critical members of the sector;

- The Treasury Department sponsored and participated in regional preparedness exercises with ChicagoFIRST members and Federal, State, and local law enforcement and first responders in July 2004, June 2005, and December 2006; and

- The Treasury Department leads quarterly testing of the emergency communications system of the FBIIC.

# 6. Measure Progress

## 6.1 CI/KR Performance Measurement

The Treasury Department, in its role as the SSA, will work with the FBIIC and the FSSCC to collect the necessary information for the descriptive, process, and outcome metrics. Because of the great diversity within the financial services sector, the Treasury Department must rely on the expertise and knowledge of the financial regulatory agencies for information on the assets within their purview.

Figure 6-1: Vulnerability Assessment Methodology

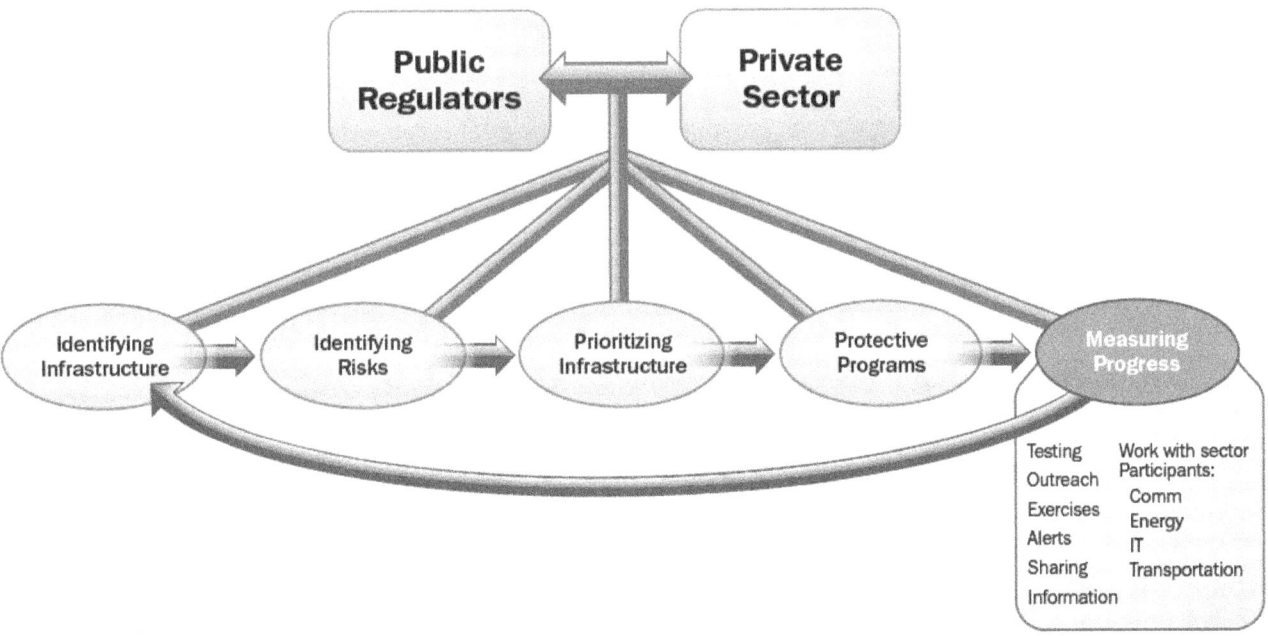

### 6.1.1 Developing Sector-Specific Metrics

As the SSA for the Banking and Finance Sector, the Treasury Department will work within the public-private partnership of the FBIIC and the FSSCC to create suitable sector metrics. Measurements of the resilience efforts in a large and diverse sector such as the Banking and Finance Sector are difficult to quantify using standard business measurements. Therefore, a one-size-fits-all approach would be inapplicable to all aspects of the sector and also would weaken creativity and vitality in the sector, which would harm the Nation's overall economy.

As evidenced by previous sections of this document, the Treasury Department has already done significant work in developing and collecting descriptive and process metrics. The Treasury Department will continue to develop and collect meaningful outcome and baseline metrics and measurements that are relevant for the sub-sectors within the Banking and Finance Sector.

The Treasury Department, working with the FBIIC and the FSSCC, has created the following process to develop metrics for the Baking and Finance Sector to address the security goals outlined in section 2.

Goal 1: To maintain its current strong position of resilience, risk management, and redundant systems in the face of a myriad of intentional, unintentional, manmade, and natural threats, the Treasury Department, as the SSA, will work with the appropriate members of the FBIIC and the FSSCC to determine:

- The appropriate number of joint meetings for the FBIIC and the FSSCC;

- The need and appropriate number of outreach meetings to financial services representatives across the country;

- The number of private sector firms that qualify under the National Security and Emergency Preparedness guidelines for GETS, WPS, and TSP;

- The level of support for regional financial partnerships;

- The level of support for RPC FIRST, the council of the regional partnerships;

- The percentage of assets that receive physical and cyber security alerts, either directly or indirectly through the FS-ISAC;

- The success of the testing schedule for the FS-ISAC's CINS;

- The appropriate coordination of the HSIN into the information-sharing structure for the sector;

- The level of participation in national and regional exercises to test and enhance the resilience of the financial services sector and level of support or outreach for such exercises;

- The portions of the sector that conduct protective-response planning exercises for critical financial infrastructures;

- The success of tests conducted to strengthen the response protocols for the FBIIC and the FSSCC;

- The portion of financial services sector participants that develop and test business continuity plans;

- The appropriate review and update processes by the Treasury Department and the FBIIC agencies for asset data on the sector;

- The appropriate level of security clearances for members of the FSSCC to participate in briefings on threats to the sector; and

- The success of the annual industry-wide business continuity planning test conducted by FSSCC members SIFMA, the Futures Industry Association (FIA), and the Financial Information Forum (FIF). These annual tests are part of an ongoing industry initiative to test the ability of primary securities market participants to operate through a significant emergency. The test, which includes both buy-side and sell-side participation, demonstrates and verifies the capacity of firms, markets, and utilities to continue functioning and communicating during an emergency by using backup sites, recovery facilities, and backup communications across the industry

Goal 2: To address and manage the risks posed by the dependence of the sector on the Communications, Information Technology, Energy, and Transportation sectors, the Treasury Department, as the SSA, will work with the appropriate members of the FBIIC and the FSSCC to determine:

- The level of collaboration with GCCs and Sector Coordinating Councils (SCC) of the Communications, Information Technology, Energy, and Transportation sectors as well as specific industry participants to identify concerns and foster information sharing regarding cross-sector vulnerabilities and protective measures;

- The level of collaboration with the NCS and other telecommunications partners to identify gaps;

- The necessary level of redundancy and assurance from the Communications, Information Technology, Energy, and Transportation sectors to meet the vision statement of the Banking and Finance Sector;

- The level of participation in and support for pandemic exercises to pinpoint areas of concern where the financial services sector depends upon the infrastructure of other sectors; and

- The level of coordination between regional coalitions and State and local emergency managers and other sector partners.

Goal 3: To advance the work of the law enforcement community, the private sector, and our international counterparts to increase the amount of available resources dedicated to tracking and catching criminals responsible for cyber attacks and other electronic crimes, the Treasury Department, as the SSA, will work with the appropriate members of the FBIIC and the FSSCC to determine:

- The level of participation and frequency of briefings between law enforcement and the financial services regulators and the private sector when specified instances of cyber and other electronic crimes arise; and

- Ways to identify and increase awareness of emerging technologies that may assist with combating cyber and electronic crime or that may be used by criminal elements to conduct cyber and electronic crime.

### 6.1.2 Information Collection and Verification

As previously stated, the Federal and State financial regulators gather a wide range of information on their regulated institutions for a variety of purposes; therefore, the Treasury Department will coordinate with the members of the FBIIC to gather appropriate core metrics information on the Banking and Finance Sector. For example, the Treasury Department will confer with the OCC for appropriate information on national banks; the NCUA for appropriate information on Federally insured credit unions; the SEC for appropriate information on investment advisors, broker/dealers, and securities markets; and the CFTC for appropriate information on futures commission merchants, commodity pool operators, and futures markets. The financial regulators regularly obtain data from their regulated entities and have appropriate protection measures in place to safeguard such information. The Treasury Department also will validate the information with the appropriate private sector participants.

Once these core metrics are identified, the Treasury Department and the FBIIC will work to create a system that can be used to assess how these metrics will be measured for the sector. This assessment will be based on regulators' extensive knowledge of the organizations within the sector, the technology employed by the sector, and the laws and regulations that apply to the sector. Furthermore, the Treasury Department and the FBIIC agencies will work directly with each entity involved with each specific metric to validate, assess, and update the metric as necessary. On an annual basis, the Treasury and the FBIIC agencies will review the assessment methodology and each metric outcome to determine whether the metric is the appropriate metric for the future.

### 6.1.3 Reporting

As the SSA for the Banking and Finance Sector, the Treasury Department will continue to work within the reporting structure identified by HSPD-7 to provide an annual sector report to DHS. The Treasury also will coordinate with DHS to provide narrative updates on the sector metrics in support of DHS status reports. The Treasury Department also will use the established public-private partnership to share the sector metrics directly with the members of the FBIIC and the FSSCC.

## 6.2 Implementation Actions

As part of the overall NIPP, the Banking and Finance SSP provides the strategy for public and private sector partners to work together to identify, prioritize, and coordinate the protection of critical infrastructure. This SSP also summarizes the extensive activities that the sector has done and continues to do to reduce vulnerabilities and share information. As the SSA, the Treasury Department has the responsibility to coordinate the implementation actions for the Banking and Finance SSP. Given the dynamic nature of the sector, the Treasury will work closely with the FBIIC, the FSSCC, and its security partners to create dynamic implementation actions that allow the SSP to be flexible and adaptive.

In the implementation matrix, each implementation action corresponds to the appropriate stage in the NIPP risk management framework. The matrix also describes the milestone for each action as well as the appropriate sector security partners who should be involved in the implementation process.

Table 6-1: Implementation Actions

| Implementation Action | Milestone | Security Partners |
|---|---|---|
| **Set Security Goals** | | |
| Establish a sector GCC | The FBIIC was established in October 2001. | The Treasury Department, the Federal and State financial regulators, and related associations |
| Establish a sector SCC | The FSSCC was created in June 2002. | The Treasury Department, the FBIIC, and private sector partners |
| Establish a sector information-sharing system. | The FS-ISAC was established in 1999. Presently, the Treasury Department and members of the FSSCC and FS-ISAC are working with DHS to coordinate the use of the HSIN. | The Treasury Department, public and private sector partners, and DHS |
| Review and refine the sector's security goals and value proposition. | Annually within the SSP review process | The Treasury Department, the FBIIC, and the FSSCC |
| **Identify Assets, Systems, Networks, and Functions** | | |
| Identify, evaluate, and update the current methodologies for validating assets, systems, and networks in the sector. | Annually | The Treasury Department, the Federal and State financial regulators, and private sector partners |

| Implementation Action | Milestone | Security Partners |
|---|---|---|
| Identify, evaluate, and update the current methodologies for validating assets, systems, and networks at the institution level. | Daily | Federal and State financial regulators and members of the private sector |
| Collect data on critical assets. | Annually | The Treasury Department, the FBIIC agencies, and private sector partners |
| Verify and review asset information. | Annually | The Treasury Department, the FBIIC agencies, and private sector partners |
| Update asset data. | As needed basis | The Treasury Department, the FBIIC agencies, and private sector partners |
| **Assess Risks** | | |
| Conduct risk assessments and mitigate vulnerabilities. | Daily per regulatory requirements | Financial regulatory authorities and the private sector |
| Develop and review risk assessment methodologies for the sector. | Annually | The Treasury Department, the FBIIC agencies, and private sector partners |
| Establish and evaluate a screening process to identify and assess critical assets, systems, and networks. | Annually | The Treasury Department, the FBIIC agencies, and private sector partners |
| Assess consequences, vulnerabilities, and threats. | As-needed basis | The Treasury Department, the FBIIC agencies, and private sector partners, DHS |
| Identify and address sector dependencies. | As-needed basis | The Treasury Department, the FBIIC agencies, and private sector partners, DHS, and other critical sectors (Energy, Information Technology, Communications, Transportation) |
| **Prioritize** | | |
| Identify and prioritize systemically important assets, processes, and networks. | Annually | The Treasury Department, the FBIIC agencies, and private sector partners |

| Implementation Action | Milestone | Security Partners |
| --- | --- | --- |
| **Implement Protective Programs** | | |
| Continue to conduct protective programs to address the sector security goals. | Ongoing basis | The Treasury Department, the FBIIC, the FSSCC, DHS, and other public and private sector partners |
| **Measure Effectiveness** | | |
| Develop appropriate descriptive, process, and outcome sector-specific metrics. | Annually | The Treasury Department, the FBIIC, and the FSSCC |

## 6.3 Challenges and Continuous Improvement

The evolving nature of the Banking and Finance Sector poses a unique challenge to the Treasury and its public and private sector partners to update these metrics continually. The Treasury Department and its public and private sector partners must remain aware of emerging technologies and vulnerabilities that the sector may face to determine whether the metrics are appropriate for the sector. Another challenge for the sector is addressing and managing the risks associated with the sector's interdependencies. As the SSA, the Treasury will continue to work with the GCCs of other sectors to mitigate these risks and collaborate on creative solutions.

In the role of the SSA, the Treasury, working with the FBIIC agencies, has the responsibility for measuring the progress of sector efforts as related to SSP. The Treasury, working with its public and private sector partners, created the stated metrics for the Banking and Finance Sector, which were designed specifically with the sector security goals in mind. These sector goals and metrics are a guiding force in the Treasury's decision making process in the role of the SSA. For instance, the Treasury, the FBIIC agencies, and members of the FSSCC work to conduct tests and exercises designed to achieve the sector security goals. These organizations also set the topics for the outreach events with these metrics and goals at the forefront. Annually, when the SSA sets forth the objectives for the Banking and Finance Sector to achieve the sector goals, the Treasury will work with the FBIIC and the FSSCC to determine whether the established metrics are the appropriate metrics. Working with its public and private sector partners, the Treasury will identify gaps in the sector metrics and security goals.

# 7. CI/KR Protection R&D

## 7.1 Overview of Sector R&D

At the request of the Treasury, the FSSCC joined DHS in a May 2005 workshop focused on R&D priorities. As DHS was finalizing the NIPP R&D plans and programs, the FSSCC formed an R&D Committee to further develop plans and programs that would provide the most significant benefits with respect to the specific CI/KR requirements of the financial services sector. In June 2006, this committee issued a list of research challenges that provide information security professionals with tools for addressing known vulnerabilities in the sector.[30]

## 7.2 Sector R&D Requirements

Extensive networks of information technology systems support the Banking and Finance Sector. These systems are composed of networks, servers, mainframes, operating systems, and software applications. The sector uses some of the most advanced technologies available to process billions of transactions each day, such as trade orders, clearing and settlements transactions, custody, account balances, and retail payments. Information systems may be rendered unavailable by either cyber or physical attacks. Compromises to the financial services sector's information technology systems may affect sector operations and public trust and confidence in the U.S. economy.

In addition to information technology systems, the Banking and Finance Sector is heavily dependent on telecommunications. Given a wide-scale disruption of the telecommunications infrastructure, the Banking and Finance Sector likely would be unable to maintain critical voice and data communications at the level necessary to assure continuity of critical operations. Because of the interdependencies of financial services sector participants, a localized disruption that impacts a systemically critical organization also may result in cascading disruptions of trading, settlement, and payment activities across the country and in foreign markets.

The FSSCC R&D Committee identified eight areas that may present significant issues to the ability of the financial sector to meet its challenges in the coming years. The areas are:

- Secure Financial Transaction Protocol (SFTP);

- Resilient Financial Transaction System (RFTS);

- Enrollment and Identity Credential Management;

- Suggested Practices and Standards;

---

[30] This document includes an appendix to the SSP entitled "FSSCC R&D Challenges."

- Understanding and Avoiding of the Insider Threat;

- Financial Information Tracing and Policy Enforcement;

- Testing; and

- Standards for Measuring Return on Investment of CIP and Security Technology.

The impact and timing of trends contributing to the challenges was assessed and recommendations made for research that would support the financial services industry through these challenges.

## 7.3 Sector R&D Plan

In 2006, the FSSCC R&D Committee began an effort to build on the sector's research challenges. The committee drafted a financial services sector research agenda demonstrating how FSSCC research challenges relate to the NIPP. It is intended that DHS should use this research agenda as input to prioritize CI/KR research supporting the Banking and Finance Sector.

An analysis of both documents indicates that there are many areas common to the NIPP and FSSCC R&D research programs and that, with minor modifications, the two programs can be synchronized to mutual benefit. Especially noteworthy are the following national R&D themes that would have the most impact on the financial services sector:

- Protection and Prevention Systems;

- Advanced Infrastructure Architecture; and

- Human and Social Issues.

The FSSCC R&D Committee recommends that research in these areas be given national priority and stands ready to assist in developing a coordinated plan through the Treasury Department and critical sectors, and the overall NIPP program. (See appendix on the FSSCC R&D Agenda.)

## 7.4 R&D Management Processes

The Treasury Department has been working with the Critical Information Infrastructure Protection (CIIP) Interagency Working Group (IWG) to draft the physical and cyber portion of the national CIP R&D strategy. The Treasury continues to exchange facts and information with numerous individuals and organizations both inside and outside the sector to identify R&D projects that will benefit the financial services sector with the goal of making the sector more resilient against external and internal threats. The Treasury Department believes that this pragmatic approach is the best method of making the sector more secure.

The FSSCC R&D Committee is organized to support R&D initiatives to ensure the protection and resilience of the physical and electronic infrastructure of the Banking and Finance Sector's activities that are vital to the Nation's economic well-being. The committee provides guidance for the creation of a FSSCC R&D Agenda to identify and prioritize areas of need. The committee also provides industry, research/academia, and the public with insights into the opportunities and requirements. Further, the committee facilitates the coordination of financial services sector-wide R&D voluntary activities and initiatives designed to improve the sector's critical infrastructure protection and homeland security.

The FSSCC R&D Committee operates with the following charter:

- Create a FSSCC R&D Agenda to identify and prioritize the areas of need so that the most promising opportunities can be found for R&D initiatives to improve the financial services sector's critical infrastructure protection significantly;

- Publish updates as needed to documentation of the FSSCC R&D Agenda, to provide industry, research/academia, and the public with a shared insight into the opportunities and requirements;

- Provide guidance for the process by which research proposals are selected and funded. Provide documentation of selection criteria and success factors used to identify the most promising proposals for funding;

- Provide the financial industry, research/academia, technologists, entrepreneurs, and the public with a better understanding of the needs and opportunities through outreach programs; and

- Coordinate support for R&D across the financial institutions represented by the FSSCC and its members, providing collaborative review of research proposals and identification of financial institutions interested in participating in the research, providing test data, and deploying results for productive use by the financial industry.

# 8. Manage and Coordinate SSA Responsibilities

## 8.1 Program Management Approach

The Secretary of the Treasury has designated the Assistant Secretary for Financial Institutions as the Treasury official with the responsibility for carrying out the Treasury's duties as the SSA for the Banking and Finance Sector. To perform these functions on a daily basis, the Assistant Secretary has designated the Office of Critical Infrastructure Protection and Compliance Policy as the lead office in fulfilling the requirements of creating the SSP for the Banking and Finance Sector. The Treasury Department will review the effectiveness of the SSP program to accomplish the SSA responsibilities.

## 8.2 Process and Responsibilities

### 8.2.1 SSP Maintenance and Update

As the SSA, the Treasury Department will work with its public and private partners, the FBIIC and the FSSCC, to review and update the SSP in coordination with the triennial review cycle of the update of the NIPP Base Plan. The Treasury Department will be the lead coordinator of the review and update cycle. At least twice during each SSP creation cycle, the Treasury Department will contact the FBIIC and the FSSCC to exchange facts and information that will enable the Treasury to determine which parts, if any, of the SSP need to be updated or modified based upon changes that have occurred within the sector. Information regarding these changes will be collected, analyzed, and managed by the Treasury Department and then, if the Treasury deems it appropriate, incorporated into the updated SSP. The updated SSP will be circulated to all the FBIIC and the FSSCC members for their individual review and comment. All changes that are made to the SSP will be forwarded to the designated DHS program office assigned to receive such changes.

### 8.2.2 Annual Reporting

The Treasury Department exchanges facts and information with the members of the FBIIC and the FSSCC in developing and updating the Banking and Finance Sector CI/KR Protection Annual Report. The Treasury Department provides the updated Banking and Finance Sector CI/KR Protection Annual Report to the appropriate DHS program office.

### 8.2.3 Training and Education

Since the majority of the Banking and Finance Sector is owned and operated by the private sector, the Treasury, the FBIIC, the FSSCC, and other sector participants continually work together to share responsibility for protecting the sector. A key component of this responsibility is education and training public and private sector participants on business continuity, information sharing, emergency response protocols, and the dependence on other sectors. As the owners and operators of the Banking and

Finance Sector, the private sector participants are responsible for establishing business continuity and protection programs. The Treasury Department and the other FBIIC members individually assist the private sector by setting policy to improve sector resilience. The FBIIC and FSSCC members also conduct FBIIC/FSSCC outreach meetings throughout the country, aimed at educating and informing the public and private sector participants about emergency response programs, cyber attacks, emergency management, and communications programs. In 2005, the FBIIC/FSSCC outreach meetings occurred in more than 25 cities, while the 2006-2007 meetings will reach 37 cities. The current meeting cycle encourages sector participants to coordinate during a crisis and promotes the idea of a regional financial coalition when the private sector participants find a need for such a mechanism.

Training and exercises are central components of maintaining the financial services sector's resilience before, during, and after an incident. The Treasury, the FBIIC, and the FSSCC work together to conduct exercises aimed at testing the preparedness and resilience of the sector. As the SSA, the Treasury routinely coordinates communications tests for information sharing between the FBIIC and the FSSCC to ensure that communications protocols will work efficiently and effectively during an incident.

The Treasury also sponsored exercises for regional financial coalitions in 2004, 2005, and 2006, such as ChicagoFIRST and FloridaFIRST, which tested the sector's resilience and response to physical threats and pandemic influenza.

The FSSCC, the FS-ISAC, and several of its members, participated in a regional exercise, Cyber Tempest, which took place in November 2006, in conjunction with several northeastern States, Government agencies, and multiple ISACs to explore interdependencies and to assure effective and efficient communications channels and protocols are in place for incident response.

In addition, the FSSCC is working with academia to develop a cyber syllabus to address specific needs of the Banking and Finance Sector's information technology infrastructure.

## 8.3 Implementing the Sector Partnership Model

All of the sector partners must work together continually to promote and maintain the sector partnership model to ensure that the sector is resilient. In the Banking and Finance Sector, the FBIIC and the FSSCC serve as the public and private participants in the sector partnership model at the national level. (See section 1.2 for details.)

Currently, the FBIIC and the FSSCC meet at least three times per calendar year in both separate sessions and joint meetings. In the separate sessions, both the FBIIC and the FSSCC conduct committee business. When the FBIIC and the FSSCC meet jointly, the committees discuss a range of issues, including emergency protocols, information-sharing mechanisms, educational programs, sector training, and the sector's dependence on other sectors. In addition to these meetings, the committee working groups meet throughout the year as is warranted based upon issues that impact the sector.

On a regional basis, financial firms across the country have formed and continue to form regional coalitions to facilitate this interaction; the regional partnerships have formed a RPC FIRST. Representatives of RPC FIRST meet quarterly and attend FSSCC meetings on a quarterly basis.

## 8.4 Information Sharing and Protection

Information sharing is an important aspect of the sector partnership model. In the Banking and Finance Sector, there are three different and complementary information-sharing mechanisms for the sector: the FBIIC, the FSSCC, and the FS-ISAC. Each of these organizations gathers information regarding the status of the sector and shares that information both within their organizations and with other organizations as appropriate. The FBIIC, the FSSCC, and the FS-ISAC have established emergency response protocols to communicate to the SSA, their members, and to each other during an incident. Furthermore, sector trade associations have developed information-sharing protocols to provide their specific members with appropriate and timely information. This information-sharing structure provides individuals with operational responsibilities as well as high-level decision makers with the appropriate information as needed.

The Treasury Department has formalized the overall collaboration of the FBIIC, the FSSCC, and the FS-ISAC. As the SSA, the Treasury Department also works with its security partners at the Federal level, including DHS, DOJ, and the law enforcement community, to share and analyze sector information. The Treasury Department is in daily contact with the FBIIC, the FSSCC, and the FS-ISAC to communicate any necessary sector information gathered from its collaboration with the security partners. For instance, one FBIIC member, the OCC, detailed an OCC employee to DHS to act as a conduit among DHS, the Treasury, the FBIIC, the FSSCC, and the FS-ISAC to coordinate information flow regarding critical infrastructure protection issues.

Figure 8-1: Information Flow

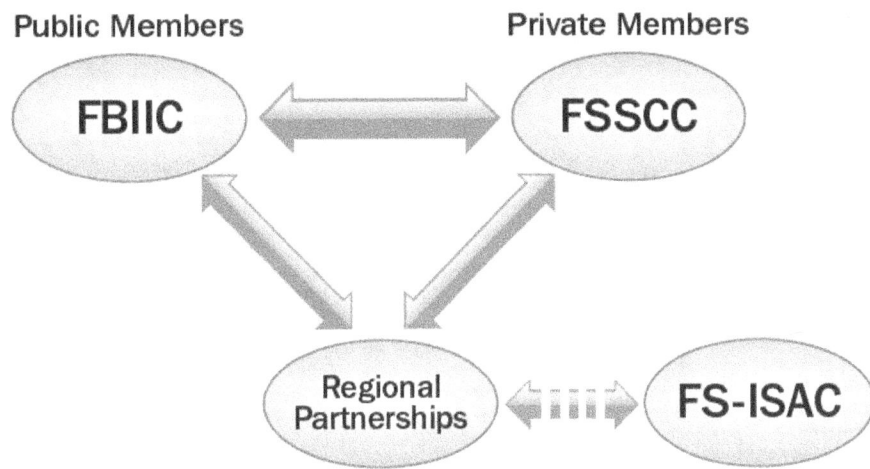

On a daily basis, the FS-ISAC reaches more than 11,000 sector participants through partnership with several FSSCC members, including the American Bankers Association, and promotes information sharing between the public and private sectors. The FS-ISAC provides sector-wide knowledge about physical and cyber security risks faced by the financial services sector. The FS-ISAC allows its members to receive threat and vulnerability information immediately; share vulnerabilities and information anonymously and communicate within a secure portal; access new data feeds of threat and vulnerability information; and access a wide range of user data from which users can produce their own reports and metrics.

The FS-ISAC's Threat and Intelligence Committee (TIC) has established a Threat Advisory Level procedure for the financial services sector that is responsive to the needs of the sector. The sector information technology security expertise of the members on the committee, representing firms comprising more than 80 percent of the capital of the sector, is utilized to set the Cyber Threat Advisory Level for cyber threats and vulnerabilities. Members of the TIC have law enforcement, military, and intelligence backgrounds, with significant experience in threat analysis and response. The Physical Threat Advisory Level is closely aligned with the DHS Homeland Security Advisory System (HSAS).

In addition, DHS has created a HSIN for the financial services sector. The FSSCC and the FS-ISAC are working with DHS to appropriately coordinate the HSIN into the information-sharing structure for the sector. The HSIN is currently one of a number of information feeds into the FS-ISAC's 24/7 Security Operations Center (SOC). Relevant information from DHS is shared downstream through the FS-ISACs notification system, and Web portal and reports from FS-ISAC members, who have approved information sharing with DHS , are uploaded through the system.

# Appendix 1: List of Acronyms and Abbreviations

| | | | | |
|---|---|---|---|---|
| **ACH** | Automated Clearinghouse | | **ESFLG** | Emergency Support Function Leader Group |
| **ASIS** | American Society for Industrial Security International | | **FBIIC** | Financial and Banking Information Infrastructure Committee |
| **ATM** | Automated Teller Machine | | **FCA** | Farm Credit Administration |
| **BARC FIRST** | Bay Area Response Coalition | | **FDIC** | Federal Deposit Insurance Corporation |
| **BCP** | Business Continuity Planning | | **FFIEC** | Federal Financial Institutions Examinations Council |
| **CFR** | Code of Federal Regulations | | **FHFB** | Federal Housing Finance Board |
| **CFTC** | Commodity Futures Trading Commission | | **FIA** | Futures Industry Association |
| **CHIPS** | Clearing House Interbank Payments System | | **FIF** | Financial Information Forum |
| **CI/KR** | Critical Infrastructure and Key Resources | | **FIRST** | Forum of Incident Response and Security Teams |
| **CINS** | Critical Infrastructure Notification System | | **FR** | Federal Register |
| **CIPAC** | Critical Infrastructure Partnership Advisory Council | | **FRB** | Board of Governors of the Federal Reserve System |
| **CIP/HLS** | Critical Infrastructure Protection and Homeland Security | | **FRB-NY** | Federal Reserve Bank of New York |
| **CME** | Chicago Mercantile Exchange | | **FS-ISAC** | Financial Services- Information Sharing and Analysis Center |
| **CSBS** | Conference of State Bank Supervisors | | **FSLC** | Federal Senior Leadership Council |
| **CSIA** | Cyber Security and Information Assurance | | **FSSCC** | Financial Services Sector Coordinating Council |
| **CSIA IWG** | Cyber Security and Information Assurance Interagency Working Group | | **FSTC** | Financial Services Technology Consortium |
| **DHS** | Department of Homeland Security | | **GCC** | Government Coordinating Council |
| **DOJ** | Department of Justice | | **GDP** | Gross Domestic Product |
| **DTCC** | Depository Trust & Clearing Corporation | | **GETS** | Government Emergency Telecommunications Service |
| **EOP** | Executive Office of the President | | **GSE** | Government-Sponsored Enterprise |
| **E.O.** | Executive Order | | | |

| | |
|---|---|
| **HIIB RFI** | Homeland Security Integrated Intelligence Board Task Force |
| **HITRAC** | Homeland Infrastructure Threat and Risk Analysis Center |
| **HSAC** | Homeland Security Advisory Council |
| **HSAS** | Homeland Security Advisory System |
| **HSC** | Homeland Security Council |
| **HSIN** | Homeland Security Information Network |
| **HSPD-7** | Homeland Security Presidential Directive 7 |
| **IDS** | Intrusion Detection System |
| **IPS** | Intrusion Prevention System |
| **IRC** | InfoSec Research Council |
| **ISAC** | Information Sharing and Analysis Center |
| **ISO** | International Organization for Standardization |
| **IT GCC** | Information Technology Government Coordinating Council |
| **IWG** | Interagency Working Group |
| **MSRB** | Municipal Securities Rulemaking Board |
| **NAIC** | National Association of Insurance Commissioners |
| **NASAA** | North American Securities Administrators Association |
| **NASCUS** | National Association of State Credit Union Supervisors |
| **NCRCG** | National Cyber Response Coordination Group |
| **NCS** | National Communications System |
| **NCUA** | National Credit Union Administration |
| **NFA** | National Futures Association |
| **NIAC** | National Infrastructure Advisory Council |
| **NIPP** | National Infrastructure Protection Plan |
| **NYBOT** | New York Board of Trade |
| **NYSE** | New York Stock Exchange |
| **OCC** | Office of Comptroller of the Currency |
| **OCIP** | U.S. Department of the Treasury, Office of Critical Infrastructure Protection and Compliance Policy |
| **OFHEO** | Office of Federal Housing Enterprise Oversight |

| | |
|---|---|
| **OMG** | Object Management Group |
| **OTS** | Office of Thrift Supervision |
| **OWASP** | Open Web Application Security Project |
| **PCII** | Protected Critical Infrastructure Information |
| **PCIS** | Partnership for Critical Infrastructure Security |
| **PDD** | Presidential Decision Directive |
| **PIN** | Personal Identification Number |
| **R&D** | Research and Development |
| **RFTS** | Resilient Financial Transaction System |
| **RPC** | Regional Partnership Council |
| **SCC** | Sector Coordinating Council |
| **SEC** | Securities and Exchange Commission |
| **SFTP** | Secure Financial Transaction Protocol |
| **SHIRA** | Strategic Homeland Infrastructure Risk Assessment |
| **SIA** | Securities Industry Association |
| **SIAC** | Securities Industry Automation Corporation |
| **SIBCMG** | Securities Industry Business Continuity Management Group |
| **SIFMA** | Securities Information and Financial Markets Association |
| **SIPC** | Securities Investor Protection Corporation |
| **SOC** | Security Operations Center |
| **SRO** | Self-Regulatory Organization |
| **SSA** | Sector-Specific Agency |
| **SSP** | Sector-Specific Plan |
| **S&T** | Science and Technology Directorate of DHS |
| **TIC** | Threat and Intelligence Committee |
| **TOPOFF** | Top Officials Exercise |
| **TSP** | Telecommunications Service Priority |
| **U.S.** | United States |
| **U.S.C.** | United States Code |
| **WPS** | Wireless Priority Service |

# Appendix 2: Statutory Authorities

The Banking and Finance Sector is subject to an extensive number of Federal and State laws and regulations. In addition, financial regulators issue guidance and white papers addressing issues of resilience, information assurance, and potential risks to institutions. Although the list cannot be exhaustive, this appendix provides a sampling of the statutes, regulations, and guidance affecting the Banking and Finance Sector.

## Statutory Authorities – Federal Regulators

### Commodity Futures Trading Commission

| U.S. Code & Regulations | Date | Subject |
| --- | --- | --- |
| 7 U.S.C. § 1, et seq. | | Commodity Exchange Act |
| 17 CFR Parts 1-190 | | Regulations of the CFTC |

### Farm Credit Administration

| U.S. Code & Regulations | Date | Subject |
| --- | --- | --- |
| 12 U.S.C.§ 2001, et seq. | 1971 | The Farm Credit Act of 1971 provides the statutory authority to regulate Farm Credit System institutions. |
| 12 CFR Parts 600-655 | | Regulations of the FCA |

## Federal Deposit Insurance Corporation

| U.S. Code & Regulations | Date | Subject |
| --- | --- | --- |
| 12 U.S.C. § 1861, et seq. | | Bank Service Company Act |
| 12 U.S.C. § 1811 | | Federal Deposit Insurance Corporation |

## Federal Financial Institutions Examination Council

| U.S. Code & Regulations | Date | Subject |
| --- | --- | --- |
| 12 U.S.C. § 3301 – § 3311 | | |
| 12 U.S.C. § 3331 – § 3352 | | Appraisal Subcommittee |

## Federal Housing Finance Board

| U.S. Code & Regulations | Date | Subject |
| --- | --- | --- |
| 12 U.S.C. § 1421, et. seq. | | The Federal Home Loan Bank Act principal statute for the Federal Housing Finance Board and Federal Home Loan Banks. |
| 12 U.S.C. § 1422a(3) | | Duties of the Federal Housing Finance Board are to ensure that the Federal Home Loan Banks operate in a safe and sound manner, and, to the extent consistent with safety and soundness, to supervise the Federal Home Loan Banks, to ensure that the Federal Home Loan Banks carry out their housing finance mission, and to ensure that the Federal Home Loan Banks remain adequately capitalized and able to raise funds in the capital markets. |
| 12 U.S.C. § 1422b | | The general powers of the Federal Housing Finance Board. |
| 12 CFR Parts 900-998 | | Rules and Regulations of the Federal Housing Finance Board that pertain to the Federal Home Loan Banks. |
| 12 CFR Part 985 | | Most of Federal Housing Finance Board's rules dealing with the Office of Finance. |

## Federal Reserve Board

| U.S. Code & Regulations | Date | Subject |
| --- | --- | --- |
| 12 U.S.C. § 248(a) | | Federal Reserve Act authorizes the Board to examine the accounts, books, and affairs of each member bank. |
| 12 U.S.C. § 1844(c) | | Bank Holding Act of 1956 authorizes the Board to examine each holding company and subsidiary (except for functionally regulated non-bank subsidiaries, e.g., registered broker dealers and insurance underwriters). |
| 12 U.S.C. § 3105 (c) | | International Banking Act of 1978 authorizes the Board to examine each branch or agency of a foreign bank. |
| 12 U.S.C. § 611, et seq. and 12 CFR § 211.13(b) | | Authorizes the Board to examine Edge and Agreement corporations. |
| 12 U.S.C. § 1861, et seq. | | Bank Service Company Act |
| 12 U.S.C. § 1867 (a) and (c) | | Bank Service Company Act authorizes the Board to examine bank service companies owned by State member-insured banks and any independent company that performs the same type of services for State member-insured banks that are authorized under the Bank Service Company Act. |

## National Credit Union Administration

| U.S. Code & Regulations | Date | Subject |
| --- | --- | --- |
| 12 U.S.C. § 1751, et seq. | | Federal Credit Union Act provides the authority for the National Credit Union Administration to regulate and insure federally and State-chartered credit unions. |
| 12 CFR Parts 700-796 | | National Credit Union Administration Rules and Regulations implement the provisions of the Federal Credit Union Act. |

## Office of Comptroller of the Currency

| U.S. Code & Regulations | Date | Subject |
| --- | --- | --- |
| 12 U.S.C. § 1, et seq. | | Charter |
| 12 U.S.C. § 2, et seq. | | National Banks |
| 12 U.S.C. § 18, et seq. | | Bank Service Company Act |

## Office of Federal Housing Enterprise Oversight

| U.S. Code & Regulations | Date | Subject |
| --- | --- | --- |
| 12 CFR Parts 1700-1780 | | Rules and Regulations of OFHEO pertaining to the Enterprises |
| 12 U.S.C., § 4501, et seq. | 1992 | The Federal Housing Enterprises Financial Safety and Soundness Act of 1992 |
| 12 U.S.C. § 4511 | | Establishes the Office of Federal Housing Enterprise Oversight |
| 12 U.S.C. §§ 4512-4526 | | Duties and Authorities of Director, OFHEO |
| 12 U.S.C. § 4611, et seq. | | Required Capital Levels for Enterprises; Enforcement Powers |

## Office of Thrift Supervision

| U.S. Code & Regulations | Date | Subject |
| --- | --- | --- |
| 12 U.S.C. 1461, et seq. | | Home Owners Loan Act authorizes OTS to examine and supervise savings associations and savings and loan holding companies. |
| 12 CFR Parts 500-591 | | Rules and Regulations of the Office of Thrift Supervision |

## Securities and Exchange Commission

| U.S. Code & Regulations | Date | Subject |
| --- | --- | --- |
| 15 U.S.C. 78a, et seq. | 1934 | Securities Exchange Act of 1934 |
| 15 U.S.C. 80a-1, et seq. | 1940 | Investment Company Act of 1940 |
| 15 U.S.C. 80b-1, et seq. | 1940 | Investment Advisers Act of 1940 |

## Securities Investor Protection Corporation*

| U.S. Code & Regulations | Date | Subject |
| --- | --- | --- |
| 15 U.S.C. 78aaa, et seq. | 1970 | The Securities Investor Protection Act of 1970 |
| 15 U.S.C. 78ccc(e)(2) | | Rules to effectuate the purpose and operations of SIPC. See 17 CFR Part 300. |
| 15 U.S.C. 78fff(b) | | Allows SIPC to conduct a liquidation proceeding "in accordance with, and as though it were being conducted under chapters 1, 3, and 5 and subchapters I and II of chapter 7" of the Bankruptcy Code, 11 U.S.C. § 101, et seq. |

\* This corporation is neither a Federal nor a State regulator; however, it was established by a Federal statute.

## Department of the Treasury

| U.S. Code & Regulations | Date | Subject |
|---|---|---|
| 12 U.S.C. 90 | | National Banks Depositories of Public Money and Financial Agents |
| 31 U.S.C. 3101 | | Public debt limit |
| 31 U.S.C. 3102 | | Bonds |
| 31 U.S.C. 3104 | | Certificates of indebtedness and treasury bills |
| 31 U.S.C. 3103 | | Notes |
| 31 U.S.C. 3105 | | Savings bonds |
| 31 U.S.C. 3121 | | Procedure |
| 31 U.S.C. 3122 | | Banks and trust companies as depositories |
| 31 U.S.C. 3123 | | Payment of obligations and interest on the public debt |
| 15 U.S.C. 78o-5 | | Government securities brokers and dealers |

## Statutory Authorities – State Regulators

### Conference of State Bank Supervisors-State Banking Departments

| State | Banking Law/Statute |
|---|---|
| Alabama | Alabama Banking Code Title 5, Chapters 1A through 13B and Chapter 20 |
| Alaska | Alaska Statutes (AS) Title 06, Banks and Financial Institutions |
| Arizona | Arizona Revised Statutes (ARS) Title 6, Banks and Financial Institutions |
| Arkansas | Arkansas Code Title 23, Subtitle 2, Financial Institutions and Securities |

| State | Banking Law/Statute |
|---|---|
| California | California Financial Code Divisions 1, 2, 5, 7 and 16, Banks and Trust Companies (Division 1), Savings Associations (Division 2), Credit Unions (Division 5), Industrial Loan Companies and Premium Finance Companies (Division 7), Issuers of Money Orders (Division 16) |
| Colorado | Colorado Revised Statutes (CRS) Title 11, Financial Institutions |
| Connecticut | The Banking Law of Connecticut, Title 36a |
| Delaware | Delaware Code Title 5, Banking |
| District of Columbia | District of Columbia Official Code Title 26, Banks and Other Financial Institutions |
| Florida | Florida Statutes Title XXXVIII, Chapters 655-667: Banks and Banking |
| Georgia | Official Code of Georgia Annotated (OCGA) Title 7, Financial Institutions Code of Georgia |
| Guam | Title 11, Guam Code Annotated (GCA), Finance and Taxation, Chapter 106, Banks |
| Hawaii | Hawaii Revised Statutes (HRS) Chapter 412, Code of Financial Institutions |
| Idaho | Idaho Statutes Title 26, Banks and Banking |
| Illinois | Illinois Compiled Statutes (ILCS) Chapter 205, Financial Regulation |
| Indiana | Indiana Code (IC) Title 28, Financial Institutions |
| Iowa | Iowa Code Chapter 524, Iowa Banking Act |
| Kansas | Kansas Statutes Annotated (K.S.A.) Chapter 9, Banking Code |
| Kentucky | Kentucky Revised Statutes (KRS) Chapter 287, Banks and Trust Companies |
| Louisiana | Louisiana Revised Statutes (R.S.) Title 6, Banks and Banking |
| Maine | Maine Revised Statutes (M.R.S.A.) Title 9-B, Financial Institutions; Also called the Maine Banking Code |

| State | Banking Law/Statute |
|---|---|
| Maryland | Maryland Annotated Code, Financial Institutions |
| Massachusetts | General Laws of Massachusetts Part I, Title XXII, Chapters 167-174 |
| Michigan | Michigan Compiled Law (MCL) Chapter 487, Financial Institutions |
| Minnesota | Minnesota Statutes 2005 Chapters 46-59, Banking |
| Mississippi | Mississippi Code of 1972, Annotated, Title 81, Banks and Financial Institutions |
| Missouri | Missouri Revised Statutes Title XXIV, Business and Financial Institutions |
| Montana | Montana Code Annotated 2005 Title 32, Financial Institutions |
| Nebraska | Nebraska Revised Statutes Chapter 8, Banks and Banking |
| Nevada | Nevada Revised Statutes (NRS) Title 55, Banks and Related Organizations |
| New Hampshire | New Hampshire Revised Statutes Annotated (NH RSA) Title XXXV, Banks and Banking; Loan Associations; Credit Unions |
| New Jersey | New Jersey Statutes Annotated (N.J.S.A.) Title 17, Corporations and Institutions for Finance and Insurance |
| New Mexico | New Mexico Statutes Annotated 1978 (NMSA 1978) Chapter 58, Financial Institutions and Regulations |
| New York | New York Banking Laws (NYBL) |
| North Carolina | North Carolina General Statutes (GS) Chapter 53, Banks |
| North Dakota | North Dakota Century Code (NDCC) Title 6, Banks and Banking |
| Ohio | Ohio Revised Code (ORS) Title XI, Financial Institutions |
| Oklahoma | Oklahoma Statutes (O.S.) Title 6, Banks and Trust Companies |
| Oregon | Oregon Revised Statutes (ORS) Title 53, Financial Institutions |

| State | Banking Law/Statute |
|-------|---------------------|
| Pennsylvania | Pennsylvania Banking Code of 1965, Unconsolidated Pennsylvania Statutes Title 7, Banks and Banking |
| Puerto Rico | Laws of Puerto Rico Annotated (L.P.R.A.) Title 7, Banking |
| Rhode Island | Rhode Island General Laws (R.I.G.L.) Title 19, Financial Institutions |
| South Carolina | South Carolina Code of Laws Title 34, Banking, Financial Institutions, and Money |
| South Dakota | South Dakota Codified Laws Title 51A, Banks and Banking |
| Tennessee | Tennessee Code Annotated (T.C.A.) Title 45, Banks and Financial Institutions |
| Texas | Texas Finance Code (TFC) Title 3, Financial Institutions and Businesses |
| Utah | Utah Code Annotated (UCA) Title 7, Financial Institutions Act |
| Vermont | Vermont Statutes Annotated (VSA) Title 8, Banking and Insurance |
| Virgin Islands | Virgin Islands Code Title 9 |
| Virginia | Code of Virginia Title 6.1, Banking and Finance |
| Washington | Revised Code of Washington (RCW) |
| West Virginia | West Virginia Code Chapter 31A, Banks and Banking; Chapter 31C, Credit Unions; Chapter 46A, Article 4, Regulated Consumer Lenders; Chapter 31, Article 17, Residential Mortgage Lender, Broker and Servicer Act; Chapter 32A, Article 2, Checks and Money Order Sales, Money Transmission Services, Transportation and Currency Exchange; Chapter 32A, Article 3, Check Cashing |
| Wisconsin | Wisconsin Statutes Chapter 138, Money and Rates of Interest; Chapter 214, Savings Banks; Chapter 215, Savings and Loans Associations; Chapter 220, Banking; Chapter 221 – State Banks; Chapter 222, Universal Banks; Chapter 223, Trust Company Banks and Other Fiduciaries; Chapter 224, Miscellaneous Banking and Financial Institutions Provisions; Chapter 428, First Lien Real Estate Loans |
| Wyoming | Wyoming Statutes (W.S.) Title 13, Banks, Banking and Finance |

# National Association of Insurance Commissioners

Below is a listing of the State statutory citations that form the basis for the regulation and taxation of the business of insurance. It should be noted that State laws often authorize State insurance regulators to publish regulations necessary to carry out the laws regulating insurers, insurance producers, and other regulated entities. For brevity, citations to these regulations are not included. Insurance regulators also inform regulated entities about regulatory matters through the issuance of bulletins, guidelines, or other informative communications. These documents also are not cited because of size limitations.

| Code & Regulations | State | URL |
|---|---|---|
| §§ 27-1-1 to 27-57-6 | AL | www.aldoi.gov/Legal/Title27.html |
| §§ 21.06.010 to 21.90.910 | AK | www.legis.state.ak.us/cgi-bin/folioisa.dll/stattx05/query=*/doc/{t9131} |
| §§ 20-101 to 20-3155 | AZ | www.azleg.state.az.us/ArizonaRevisedStatutes.asp?Title=20 |
| §§ 23-60-101 to 23-103-316 | AR | www.arkleg.state.ar.us/NXT/gateway.dll?f=templates&fn=default.htm&vid=blr:code<br><br>Click on "+" for Arkansas Code, then click "+" for Title 23, Subtitle 3 to view/obtain entire code. |
| Ins. §§ 1 to 16030 | CA | www.leginfo.ca.gov/.html/ins _ table _ of _ contents.html Title 10 Insurance |
| §§ 10-1-101 to 10-20-120  §§10-21-101 to 10-21-106 Repealed in 2004 (Colorado Health Care Coverage Act) | CO | http://198.187.128.12/colorado/lpext.dll?f=templates&fn=fs-main.htm&2.0<br><br>Open Statutes, click on Title 10 Insurance folder to view/obtain entire code. |
| §§ 38a-1 to 38a-1050 | CT | www.cga.ct.gov/2005/pub/Title38a.htm?cidNav=\| |
| Title 18, §§ 101 to 8014 | DE | www.delcode.state.de.us/title18/index.htm#TopOfPage |
| §§ 31-101 to 31-5608.04 | DC | http://198.187.128.12/dc/lpext.dll?=templates&fn=fs-main.htm&2.0<br><br>Open Division V Local Business Affairs, click on Title 31 Insurance and Securities to view/obtain code. |
| §§ 624.01 to 651.134 | FL | www.flsenate.gov/Statutes/index.cfm?App_mode=Display_Index&Title_Request=XXXVII#TitleXXXVII |
| §§ 33-1-1 to 33-61-2 | GA | www.legis.ga.gov/legis/GaCode/?title=33 |

| Code & Regulations | State | URL |
| --- | --- | --- |
| §§ 431:1-100 to 431:30-124 | HI | www.capitol.hawaii.gov/hrscurrent/vol09_ch0431-0435e/hrs0431/hrs_0431-.htm<br><br>This link is to a list. Click on "Next" to view individual statutes.<br><br>www.hawaii.gov/dcca/areas/ins/main/hrs (listing of statutes pertaining to insurance) |
| §§ 41-101 to 41-5702 | ID | www3.state.id.us/idstat/TOC/41FTOC.html |
| 215 ILCS 5/1 to 215 ILCS 165/30 | IL | www.ilga.gov/legislation/ilcs/ilcs5.asp?ActID=1249&ChapAct=215%26nbsp%3BILCS%26nbsp%3B5%2F&ChapterID=22&ChapterName=INSURANCE&ActName=Illinois+Insurance+Code%2E |
| IC 27-1-1-1 to 27-17-14-2 | IN | www.in.gov/legislative/ic/code/title27 |
| §§ 505.1 to 523I.814 | IA | http://coolice.legis.state.ia.us/Cool-ICE/default.asp?category=billinfo&service=Iowa Code<br><br>Type 505 to begin viewing statutes. |
| §§ 40-101 to 40-5301 | KS | www.kslegislature.org/legsrv-statutes/articlesList.do<br><br>Under Statute Table of Contents, click on Chapter 40 Insurance. |
| §§ 304.1-010 to 304.99-152 | KY | www.lrc.ky.gov/KRS/304-01/CHAPTER.HTM<br><br>Will need to click on "next chapter" to continue viewing. |
| R.S. §§ 22:1 to 22:3205 | LA | www.legis.state.la.us/lss/lss.asp?folder=1<br><br>Click on Title 22 Insurance. |
| Title 24-A §§ 1 to 6971<br>Title 24, §§ 1 to 3307 | ME | http://janus.state.me.us/legis/statutes/24-A/title24-Ach0sec0.html<br><br>http://janus.state.me.us/legis/statutes/24/title24ch0sec0.html |
| Ins. §§ 1-101 to 29-102 | MD | www.dsd.state.md.us/comar/Annot_Code_Idx/InsuranceIndex.htm |
| §§ 175:1 to 175:225; §§ 175A:1 to 175K:16 | MA | www.mass.gov/legis/laws/mgl/gl-175-toc.htm |

| Code & Regulations | State | URL |
|---|---|---|
| §§ 500.100 to 500.8302  §§ 550.1 to 550.2009 | MI | www.legislature.mi.gov/(S(gn34nh45ga0dggjhhil4ll45))/mileg.aspx?page=getObject&objectName=mcl-Act-218-of-1956<br><br>www.legislature.mi.gov/(S(gn34nh45ga0dggjhhil4ll45))/mileg.aspx?page=getobject&objectname=mcl-chap550 |
| §§ 59A.01 to79A.32 | MN | http://ros.leg.mn/stats/59A.html |
| §§ 83-1-1 to 83-67-5 | MS | http://198.187.128.12/mississippi/lpext.dll?f=templates&fn=fs-main.htm&2.0<br><br>Click on Code, then "more" to locate Title 83 Insurance. |
| §§ 374.010 to 385.080 | MO | www.moga.mo.gov/statutes/chapters/chap374.htm<br><br>www.moga.mo.gov/STATUTES/STATUTES.HTM |
| §§ 33-1-101 to 33-38-108 | MT | http://data.opi.state.mt.us/bills/mca_toc/33.htm |
| §§ 44-101 to 44.8107 | NE | http://uniweb.legislature.ne.gov/legaldocs/search.php<br><br>Scroll down to "View All" and select 44-Insurance from drop down. |
| §§ 679A.010 to 697.370 | NV | www.leg.state.nv.us/NRS/NRS-679A.html<br><br>www.leg.state.nv.us/NRS/Index.cfm |
| §§ 400-A:1 to 420-K:7 | NH | www.gencourt.state.nh.us/rsa/html/NHTOC/NHTOC-XXXVII.htm |
| §§ 17:1-1 to 17B:36-4 | NJ | http://lis.njleg.state.nj.us/cgi-bin/om_isapi.dll?clientID=57988753&Depth=2&depth=2&expandheadings=on&headingswithhits=on&hitsperheading=on&infobase=statutes.nfo&record={52AB}&softpage=Doc_Frame_PG42 |
| §§ 59A-1-1 to 59A-59-4 | NM | www.conwaygreene.com/nmsu/lpext.dll?f=templates&fn=main-h.htm&2.0<br><br>Open folder, New Mexico Statutes and Court, then click on Statutory Chapters in N.M. Statutes, then select 59A. Insurance Code.  Ins. Law |
| §§ 101 to 9901 | NY | www.ins.state.ny.us/regclinx.htm<br><br>Scroll down to New York State Consolidated Laws – Insurance link and follow directions to open link. |
| §§ 58-1-1 to 58-91-80 | NC | www.ncga.state.nc.us/EnactedLegislation/Statutes/HTML/ByChapter/Chapter_58.html |

| Code & Regulations | State | URL |
|---|---|---|
| §§ 26.1-01-01 to 26.1-53-09 | ND | www.legis.nd.gov/cencode/t261.html |
| §§ 3901.01 to 3999.99 | OH | http://onlinedocs.andersonpublishing.com/oh/lpExt.dll?f=templates&fn=main-h.htm&cp=PORC<br><br>Scroll down to Title XXXIX Insurance. |
| 36, §§ 101 to 7004 | OK | www.oscn.net/applications/oscn/index.asp?level=1&ftdb=STOKST36&level=1 |
| §§ 731.004 to 752.055 | OR | www.oregoninsurance.org/lawsrules.html<br><br>Click on Insurance Laws of Oregon 2005 link. |
| §§ 40-1-011 to 40-6335 | PA | http://members.aol.com/DKM1/40.html |
| Title 26, §§ 101 to 8061 | PR | www.michie.com<br><br>Select Jurisdiction of Puerto Rico, will need to obtain a free password/id to access Puerto Rico's code.. |
| §§ 27-1-1 to 27-69-6 | RI | www.rilin.state.ri.us/Statutes/TITLE27/INDEX.HTM |
| §§ 38-1-10 to 38-93-60 | SC | www.scstatehouse.net/code/titl38.htm |
| §§ 58-1-1 to 58-46-26 | SD | http://legis.state.sd.us/statutes/DisplayStatute.aspx?Type=Statute&Statute=58 |
| §§ 56-1-101 to 56-57-106 | TN | http://198.187.128.12/tennessee/lpext.dll?f=templates&fn=fs-main.htm&2.0<br><br>Open Tennessee Code, open "more," then select Title 56 Insurance. |
| I.C. Art. 1.01 to 29.14;<br>Ins. §§ 30.001 to 5001.002 | TX | http://tlo2.tlc.state.tx.us/statutes/in.toc.htm |
| §§ 31A-1-101 to 31A-39-101 | UT | www.le.state.ut.us/~code/TITLE31A/TITLE31A.htm |
| Title 8, §§ 3301 to 8517 | VT | www.leg.state.vt.us/statutes/chapters.cfm?Title=08 |
| Title 22, §§ 1 to 1728 | VI | http://198.187.128.12/virginislands/lpext.dll?f=templates&fn=fs-main.htm&2.0<br><br>Open V.I. Code, open "more," then select Title 22 Insurance. |

| Code & Regulations | State | URL |
|---|---|---|
| §§ 38.2-100 to 38.2-6201 | VA | http://leg1.state.va.us/000/reg/TOC14005.HTM |
| §§ 48.01.010 to 48.140.080 | WA | http://apps.leg.wa.gov/rcw/default.aspx?Cite=48 |
| §§ 33-1-1 to 33-48-12 | WV | www.legis.state.wv.us/WVCODE/33/masterfrmFrm.htm |
| §§ 600.01 to 655.68 | WI | www.legis.state.wi.us/rsb/Statutes.html  Scroll down to Insurance. |
| §§ 26-1-101 to 26-50-109 | WY | http://legisweb.state.wy.us/statutes/statutes.aspx?file=titles/Title26/Title26.htm |

## North American Securities Administrators Association

| State | Statute |
|---|---|
| Alabama | AL Code 1975, §§ 8-6-1 to 8-6-33 |
| Alaska | AK St. §§ 45.55.010 to 45.55.955 |
| Arizona | A.R.S. §§ 44-1801 to 44-2126 |
| Arkansas | A.C.A. §§ 23-42-101 to 23-42-509 |
| California | CA CORP §§ 25000 to 25707 |
| Colorado | CO ST §§11-51-101 to 11-51-908 |
| Connecticut | CT ST §§ 36b-2 to 36b-33 |
| Delaware | 6 Del.C. §§ 7301 to 7330 |
| District of Columbia | DC ST §§ 31-5601.01 to 31-5608.04 |
| Florida | FL ST §§ 517.011 to 517.32 |

| State | Statute |
|---|---|
| Georgia | GA ST §§ 10-5-1 to 10-5-24 |
| Hawaii | HI ST §§ 485-1 to 485-25 |
| Idaho | ID ST §§ 30-14-101 to 30-14-703 |
| Illinois | 815 ILCS §§ 5/1 to 5/19 |
| Indiana | IN ST §§ 23-2-1-27 |
| Iowa | IA ST §§ 502.101 to 502.701 |
| Kansas | KS ST §§ 17-12a101 to 17-12a703 |
| Kentucky | KY ST §§ 292.310 to 292.550, 292.991 |
| Louisiana | LA. R.S. §§ 701 to 724 |
| Maine | 32 M.R.S.A. §§ 16101 to 16702 |
| Maryland | MD Code, Corporations and Associations, §§ 11-101 to 11-805 |
| Massachusetts | M.G.L.A. c. 110A, §§ 101 to 417 |
| Michigan | MI ST §§ 451.501 to 451.818 |
| Minnesota | MN ST §§ 80A.01 to 80A.31 |
| Mississippi | MS Code 1972, §§ 75-71-101 to 75-71-735 |
| Missouri | V.A.M.S. §§ 409.1-101 to 409.7-703 |
| Montana | MCA §§ 30-10-101 to 30-10-308 |

| State | Statute |
| --- | --- |
| Nebraska | NE ST §§ 8-1101 to 8-1123 |
| Nevada | NV ST §§ 90.211 to 90.860 |
| New Hampshire | NH ST §§ 421-B:1 to 421-B:34 |
| New Jersey | NJ ST §§ 49:3-47 to 49:3-76 |
| New Mexico | N.M.S.A. §§ 46-8-1 to 46-8-10 |
| New York | NY ST §§ 352 to 359-h |
| North Carolina | NC ST §§ 78A-1 to 78A-66 |
| North Dakota | NDCC §§ 10-04-01 to 10-04-20 |
| Ohio | OH ST §§ 1707.01 to 1707.99 |
| Oklahoma | OK ST T. 71 §§ 1-101 to 1-701 |
| Oregon | OR ST §§ 59.005 to 59.451, 59.991, 59.995 |
| Pennsylvania | 70 P.S. §§ 1-101 to 1-704 |
| Puerto Rico | 10 L.P.R.A. §§ 851 to 895 |
| Rhode Island | RI ST 7-11-101 to 7-11-806 |
| South Carolina | SC Code 1976, §§ 35-1-101 to 35-1-703 |
| South Dakota | SDCL §§ 47-31B-101 to 47-31B-703 |
| Tennessee | TN ST. §§ 48-2-101 to 48-2-117 |
| Texas | TX CIV ST ART 581-1 to 581-60a |

| State | Statute |
|---|---|
| Utah | UT ST § 61-1-1 to 61-1-30 |
| Vermont | VT ST T.9 §§ 5101 to 5612 |
| Virginia | Va. Code 1950, §§ 13.1-501 to 13.1-527.3 |
| Washington | RCWA §§ 21.20.005 to 21.20.940 |
| West Virginia | W. Va. Code §§ 32-1-101 to 32-1-418 |
| Wisconsin | WI ST §§ 551.01 to 551.67 |
| Wyoming | WY ST §§ 17-4-101 to 17-4-131 |

## Guidance and Key Documents: Federal Regulators

### Federal Deposit Insurance Corporation

FDIC Documents: Most available online at: www.fdic.gov

See also: Examinations: Information Systems and E-Banking at www.fdic.gov/regulations/information/index.html and www.fdic.gov/regulations/information/fils/index.htm

| Date | Title | URL |
|---|---|---|
| 08-06 | Authentication in an Internet Banking Environment FAQs | www.fdic.gov/news/news/financial/2006/fil06077.html |
| 06-06 | Foreign-Based Third-Party Service Providers Guidance on Managing Risks in These Outsourcing Relationships | www.fdic.gov/news/news/financial/2006/fil06052.html |
| 03-06 | Influenza Pandemic Preparedness | www.fdic.gov/news/news/financial/2006/fil06025.html |
| 10-05 | Authentication in an Internet Banking Environment | www.fddic.gov/news/news/financial/2005/fil10305.html |
| 10-05 | Relationship Manager Program Enhancements to the Supervision Program | www.fdic.gov/news/news/financial/2005/fil9805.html |

| Date | Title | URL |
|---|---|---|
| 08-05 | Information Technology Risk Management Program (IT-RMP) New Information Technology Examination Procedures | www.fdic.gov/news/news/financial/2005/fil8105.html |
| 07-05 | Guidance on the Security Risks of VoIP | www.fdic.gov/news/news/financial/2005/fil6905.html |
| 07-05 | Guidance on Mitigating Risks from Spyware | www.fdic.gov/news/news/financial/2005/fil6605.html |
| 07-05 | "PHARMING": Guidance on How Financial Institutions Can Protect Against Pharming Attacks | www.fdic.gov/news/news/financial/2005/fil6405a.html |
| 07-05 | Guidance on How Financial Institutions Can Protect Against Pharming Attacks | www.fdic.gov/news/news/financial/2005/fil6405.html |
| 07-05 | Identity Theft Supplement on "Account-Hijacking" Identity Theft | www.fdic.gov/news/news/financial/2005/fil5905.html |
| 04-05 | Guidance on Response Programs for Unauthorized Access to Customer Information and Customer Notice | www.fdic.gov/news/news/financial/2005/fil2705.html |
| 02-05 | Fair and Accurate Credit Transactions Act of 2003 Guidelines Requiring the Proper Disposal of Consumer Information | www.fdic.gov/news/news/financial/2005/fil705.html |
| 12-04 | Identity Theft Study on "Account-Hijacking" Identity Theft and Suggestions for Reducing Online Fraud | www.fdic.gov/news/news/financial/2004/fil13204.html |
| 11-04 | Computer Software Due Diligence FAQs | www.fdic.gov/news/news/financial/2004/fil12104a.html |
| 11-04 | Computer Software Due Diligence Guidance on Developing an Effective Computer Software Evaluation Program to Assure Quality and Regulatory Compliance | www.fdic.gov/news/news/financial/2004/fil12104.html |
| 10-04 | Check Clearing for the 21st Century Act Final Amendments to the Federal Reserve Board's Regulation CC | www.fdic.gov/news/news/financial/2004/fil11604.html |
| 10-04 | Risk Management of Free and Open Source Software FFIEC Guidance | www.fdic.gov/news/news/financial/2004/fil11404.html |

| Date | Title | URL |
|---|---|---|
| 09-04 | Internet Banking Fraud | www.fdic.gov/news/news/financial/2004/fil10304.html |
| 07-04 | Guidance on the Risks Associated with Instant Messaging | www.fdic.gov/news/news/financial/2004/fil8404.html |
| 06-04 | Guidance on Developing an Effective Computer Virus Protection Program | www.fdic.gov/news/news/financial/2004/fil6204.html |
| 05-04 | Check Clearing for the 21st Century Act | www.fdic.gov/news/news/financial/2004/fil5404.html |
| 03-04 | Guidance on Safeguarding Customers Against E-Mail and Internet-Related Fraudulent Schemes | www.fdic.gov/news/news/financial/2004/fil2704.html |
| 08-03 | Guidance on Identity Theft Response Programs | www.fdic/gov/news/news/financial/2003/fil0363.html |
| 05-03 | Computer Software Patch Management | www.fdic.gov/news/news/financial/2003/fil10343.html |
| 04-03 | Weblinking | www.fdic.gov/news/news/financial/2003/fil0330.html |
| 02-03 | New Information Security Guidance for Examiners and Financial Institutions | www.fdic.gov/news/news/financial/2003/fil0311.html |
| 08-02 | Financial and Banking Information Infrastructure Committee's Interim Policy on the Sponsorship of Private Sector Financial Institutions in the GETS Card Program | www.fdic.gov/news/news/financial/2002/fil0284.html |
| 10-02 | New Examination Procedures for Assessing Information Technology Risk | www.fdic.gov/news/news/financial/2002/FIL02118.html |
| 02-02 | Guidance on Managing Risks Associated With Wireless Networks and Wireless Customer Access | www.fdic.gov/news/news/financial/2002/fil0208.html |
| 08-01 | Authentication in an Electronic Banking Environment | www.fdic.gov/news/news/financial/2001/fil0169.html |
| 08-01 | Lifting of Mandatory Compliance Date for Interim Rules Amending Regulations B, E, M, Z, and DD | www.fdic.gov/news/news/financial/2001/fil0166.html |

| Date | Title | URL |
|---|---|---|
| 08-01 | Examination Procedures to Evaluate Customer Information Safeguards | www.fdic.gov/news/news/financial/2001/fil0168.html |
| 08-01 | FDIC Seeks Comment on Study of Banking Regulations Regarding the Online Delivery of Banking Services | www.fdic.gov/news/news/financial/2001/fil0170.html |
| 08-01 | Federal Financial Institutions Examination Council CD-ROM on Financial Privacy and Information Security | www.fdic.gov/news/news/financial/2001/fil0173.html |
| 06-01 | Bank Technology Bulletin on Outsourcing | www.fdic.gov/news/news/financial/2001/fil0150.html |
| 05-01 | Guidance on Identity Theft and Pretext Calling | www.fdic.gov/news/news/financial/2001/fil0139.html |
| 05-01 | Interim Final Rules Amending Regulations B, E, M, Z, and DD Regarding Electronic Delivery of Required Disclosure | www.fdic.gov/news/news/financial/2001/fil0140.html |
| 04-01 | FFIEC's Risk Management Planning Seminar for 2001 | www.fdic.gov/news/news/financial/2001/fil0129.html |
| 04-01 | Electronic Funds Transfer | www.fdic.gov/news/news/financial/2001/fil0133.html |
| 03-01 | Electronic Funds Transfer | www.fdic.gov/news/news/financial/2001/fil0125.html |
| 03-01 | Security Standards for Customer Information | www.fdic.gov/news/news/financial/2001/fil0122.html |
| 11-00 | Risk Management of Technology Outsourcing | www.fdic.gov/news/news/financial /2000/fil0081.html |
| 11-00 | Protecting Internet Domain Names | www.fdic.gov/news/news/financial/2000/fil0077.html |
| 11-00 | Electronic Signatures in Global and National Commerce Act | www.fdic.gov/news/news/financial/2000/fil0072.html |
| 10-00 | Security Monitoring of Computer Networks | www.fdic.gov/news/news/financial/2000/fil0067.html |
| 09-00 | Digital Signatures Deployment Issues | www.fdic.gov/regulations/information/fils/banktechbulletin.html |

| Date | Title | URL |
|---|---|---|
| 09-00 | Consumer Brochure on Online Banking | www.fdic/gov/news/news/financial/2000/fil0063.html |
| 07-00 | Suspicious Activity Report | www.fdic.gov/news/news/financial/2000/fil0048.html |
| 07-00 | Proposed Security Standards for Customer Information | www.fdic.gov/news/news/financial/2000/fil0043.html |
| 02-99 | Uniform Rating System for Information Technology | www.fdic.gov/news/news/financial/1999/fil9912.html |
| 12-99 | Financial Institution Web Site Privacy Survey | www.fdic.gov/news/news/financial/1999/fil99113.html |
| 07-99 | Risk Assessment Tools and Practices for Information Security | www.fdic.gov/news/news/financial/1999/fil9968.html |
| 06-99 | Bank Service Company Act | www.fdic.gov/news/news/financial/1999/fil9949.html |
| 09-98 | Pretext Phone Calling | www.fdic.gov/news/news/financial/1998/fil9898.html |
| 08-98 | Electronic Commerce and Consumer Privacy | www.fdic.gov/news/news/financial/1998/fil9886.html |
| 07-98 | Electronic Financial Services and Consumer Compliance | www.fdic.gov/news/news/financial/1998/fil9879.html |
| 12-97 | Security Risks Associated with the Internet | www.fdic.gov/news/news/financial/1997/fil971313.html |
| 12-97 | Suspicious Activity Reporting – Computer-Related Crimes | www.fdic.gov/news/news/financial/1997/fil97124.html |
| 10-96 | Risks Involving Client/Server Computer Systems | www.fdic.gov/news/news/financial/1996/fil9682.html |

**Federal Financial Institution Examination Council** and other jointly issued documents: Available online at www.ffiec.gov/ guides.htm or the other Web sites listed.

| Date | Title | URL |
|---|---|---|
| 07-06 | FFIEC Information Security Booklet | www.occ.treas.gov/ftp/bulletin/2006-32.doc |
| 07-06 | Information Security Booklet | www.ffiec.gov/ffiecinfobase/html_pages/infosec_book_frame.htm |
| 06-06 | Lessons Learned from Hurricane Katrina: Preparing Your Institution for a Catastrophic Event | www.ffiec.gov/katrina_lessons.htm |
| 03-06 | Influenza Pandemic Preparedness<br><br>Note: This was a joint issuance by the FRB, OCC, and OCC. NCUA issued substantially equivalent guidance in March 2006 (see the NCUA section below). | www.occ.treas.gov/ftp/bulletin/2006-35.doc |
| 12-04 | FFIEC Information Technology Examination Handbook | www.federalreserve.gov/boarddocs/srletters/2004/sr0420.htm |
| 12-04 | FFIEC Guidance on the Use of Free and Open Source Software | www.federalreserve.gov/boarddocs/srletters/2004/sr0417.htm |
| 10-04 | FFIEC Brochure with Information on Internet "Phishing" | www.federalreserve.gov/boarddocs/srletters/2004/sr0414.htm |
| 9-04 | Federal Bank, Thrift and Credit Union Regulatory Agencies Provide Brochure with Information on Internet "Phishing" | www.occ.treas.gov/Consumer/phishing.htm |
| 10-03<br>01-03<br>04-04 | FFIEC Information Technology Handbook | www.ffiec.gov/ffiecinfobase/html_pages/it_01.html<br><br>www.occ.treas.gov/ftp/bulletin/2003-41.doc<br><br>www.ots.treas.gov/docs./25182.pdf<br><br>www.ncua.gov/ref/letters/2003/03-CU-07.doc |
| 07-04 | FFIEC Management Booklet | www.ffiec.gov/ffiecinfobase/html_pages/it_01.html - management<br><br>http://occnet.occ/examinerlibrary/bulletin/2004-32a. pdf |

| Date | Title | URL |
|---|---|---|
| 07-04 | FFIEC Outsourcing Technology Services Booklet | www.ffiec.gov/ffiecinfobase/html_pages/it_01.html - outsourcing<br><br>http://occnet.occ/examinerlibrary/bulletin/2004-32a. pdf |
| 07-04 | FFIEC Operations Booklet | www.ffiec.gov/ffiecinfobase/html_pages/it_01.html#operation |
| 07-04 | FFIEC Wholesale Payment Systems Booklet | www.ffiec.gov/ffiecinfobase/html_pages/it_01.html#whole |
| 06-04 | FFIEC Management Booklet | www.ffiec.gov/ffiecinfobase/html_pages/it_01.html - management |
| 06-04 | FFIEC Outsourcing Technology Services Booklet | www.ffiec.gov/ffiecinfobase/html_pages/it_01.html - outsourcing |
| 04-04 | FFIEC Development and Acquisition Booklet | www.ffiec.gov/ffiecinfobase/html_pages/it_01.html#d _a |
| 03-04 | FFIEC Retail Payments Booklet | www.ffiec.gov/ffiecinfobase/html_pages/it_01.html#rps |
| 08-03 | FFIEC Booklet on Audit Guidance | www.ffiec.gov/ffiecinfobase/booklets/audit/audit.pdf<br><br>www.occ.treas.gov/ftp/bulletin/2003-41.doc |
| 08-03 | FIEC Booklet on E-Banking Guidance | www.ffiec.gov/ffiecinfobase/booklets/e_banking/e_banking.pdf<br><br>www.occ.treas.gov/ftp/bulletin/2003-41.doc |
| 08-03 | FFIEC Booklet on Fedline Booklet Guidance | www.ffiec.gov/ffiecinfobase/booklets/fedline/fedline.pdf www.occ. treas.gov/ftp/bulletin/2003-41.doc |
| 08-03 | FFIEC E-Banking Booklet | www.ffiec.gov/ffiecinfobase/html_pages/it_01.html#ebank |
| 08-03 | FFIEC Audit Booklet | www.ffiec.gov/ffiecinfobase/html_pages/it_01.html#audit |
| 07-03<br>05-03 | New Suspicious Activity Report | http://fincen.gov/f9022-47-1a.pdf<br><br>www.fdic.gov/news/news/financial/2003/fil0356.html<br><br>www.federalreserve.gov/boarddocs/SRLETTERS/2003/sr0312.htm |

| Date | Title | URL |
|---|---|---|
| 03-31 | FFIEC Retail Payments Booklet | www.occ.treas.gov/ftp/bulletin/2004-14.doc  www.fdic.gov/news/news/financial/2003/FIL0383.html |
| 03-03<br>04-03<br>06-03 | FFIEC Business Continuity Planning Booklet | www.ffiec.gov/ffiecinfobase/html_pages/it_01.html - bcp<br><br>www.fdic.gov/news/news/financial/2003/FIL0340.html<br><br>www.occ.treas.gov/ftp/bulletin/2003-18.doc<br><br>www.ots.treas.gov/docs/25176.pdf |
| 03-03<br>04-03<br>06-03 | FFIEC Booklet on Supervision of Technology Service Providers | www.ffiec.gov/ffiecinfobase/html_pages/it_01.html#tsp<br><br>www.fdic.gov/news/news/financial/2003/FIL0340.html<br><br>www.occ.treas.gov/ftp/bulletin/2003-18.doc<br><br>www.ots.treas.gov/docs/25176.pdf |
| 04-03 | Weblinking: Identifying Risks and Risk Management Techniques | www.ffiec.gov/ffiecinfobase/resources/elect_bank/fdi-fil-30-2003_weblinking.pdf<br><br>www.fdic.gov/news/news/financial/2003/FIL0330.html<br><br>www.occ.treas.gov/ftp/bulletin/2003-15.doc<br><br>www.ots.treas.gov/docs/84263.pdf  www.ncua.gov/ref/letters/2003/03-CU-08.doc |
| 04-03 | Regulators Issue Interagency Paper on Sound Practices to Strengthen the Resilience of the U.S. Financial System | www.federalreserve.gov/boarddocs/press/bcreg/2003/20030408/default.htm<br><br>www.federalreserve.gov/boarddocs/SRLETTERS/2003/sr0309.htm<br><br>www.occ.treas.gov/ftp/bulletin/2003-14.doc |
| 03-03 | Financial and Banking Information Infrastructure Committee Policy on Sponsorship of Telecommunications Service Priority for Private Sector Entities | www.fbiic.gov/policies/TSP_policy.htm<br><br>www.occ.treas.gov/ftp/bulletin/2003-13.doc |
| 12-02 | FFIEC Booklet on Information Security Guidance for Examiners and Financial Institutes | www.ffiec.gov/ffiecinfobase/booklets/information_secruity/information_security.pdf<br><br>www.fdic.gov/news/news/financial/2003/FIL0311.html<br><br>www.occ.treas.gov/ftp/bulletin/2003-4.doc |

| Date | Title | URL |
|---|---|---|
| 08-02 | Financial and Banking Information Infrastructure Committee's Interim Policy on the Sponsorship of Private Sector Financial Institutions in the GETS Card Program | www.fbiic.gov/gets.htm<br><br>www.fdic.gov/news/news/financial/2002/fil0284.html<br><br>www.occ.treas.gov/ftp/bulletin/2002-33.doc |
| 05-01 | Safeguarding Customer Information | www.federalreserve.gov/boarddocs/SRLETTERS/2001/sr0115.htm |
| 03-00 | Lessons Learned from Y2K | www.ffiec.gov/press/pr032100.htm<br><br>www.federalreserve.gov/boarddocs/SRLETTERS/2000/SR0005.HTM<br><br>www.occ.treas.gov/ftp/advisory/2000-2.doc |
| 07-98 | Interagency Guidance on Electronic Financial Services and Consumer Compliance | www.ffiec.gov/PDF/EFS.pdf<br><br>www.fdic.gov/news/news/financial/1998/fil9879.html<br><br>www.occ.treas.gov/ftp/bulletin/98-31.txt www.ots.treas.gov/docs/25090.pdf<br><br>www.ncua.gov/ref/reg_alerts/98-RA-4.pdf |
| 07-98 | FFIEC Guidance on Electronic Financial Services and Consumer Compliance | www.occ.treas.gov/ftp/bulletin/98-31.txt |
| 4-97 | Interagency Statement on Retail On-Line Banking | www.ffiec.gov/ffiecinfobase/resources/info_sec/ncu-97_cu_5_inter-agency_statement_retail_online_bank-1997-04.pdf<br><br>www.ncua.gov/ref/letters/97-cu-5.html |

**Federal Reserve Board:** Most available online at www.federalreserve.gov.

| Date | Title | URL |
|---|---|---|
| 08-06 | Questions and Answers Related to Interagency Guidance on Authentication in an Internet Banking Environment | www.federalreserve.gov/boarddocs/srletters/2006/SR0613.htm |
| 07-06 | FFIEC Information Security Booklet | www.federalreserve.gov/boarddocs/srletters/2006/SR0612.htm |
| 03-06 | Influenza Pandemic Preparedness | www.federalreserve.gov/boarddocs/srletters/2006/SR0605.htm |

| Date | Title | URL |
|---|---|---|
| 12-05 | Interagency Guidance on Response Programs for Unauthorized Access to Customer Information and Customer Notice | www.federalreserve.gov/boarddocs/srletters/2005/sr0523.htm |
| 11-05 | Revised Training Program for Information Technology Examiners | www.federalreserve.gov/boarddocs/srletters/2005/sr0522.htm |
| 10-05 | Interagency Guidance on Authentication in an Internet Banking Environment | www.federalreserve.gov/boarddocs/srletters/2005/sr0519.htm |
| 12-04 | Final Rules on Disposal of Consumer Information Derived from Credit Reports | www.federalreserve.gov/boarddocs/press/bcreg/2004/20041221/default.htm |
| 05-03 | Interagency Paper on Sound Practices to Strengthen the Resilience of the U.S. Financial System | www.federalreserve.gov/boarddocs/srletters/2003/sr0309.htm |
| 05-01 | Safeguarding Customer Information | www.federalreserve.gov/boarddocs/SRLETTERS/2001/sr0115.htm |
| | Bank Holding Company Supervision Manual | Section 2124.4 – This new section includes the federal banking agency interagency guidelines establishing standards for safeguarding customer information (the guidelines).<br><br>www.federalreserve.gov/boarddocs/supmanual/default.htm#bhcsm |
| | Commercial Bank Examination Manual | Section 4060 revised to include GLBA 501(b) Requirements for Safeguarding Customer Information.<br><br>Section 4063 added new section – Electronic Banking to aid in the review of Internet banking activities.<br><br>www.federalreserve.gov/boarddocs/supmanual/default.htm#cbem |
| 04-01 | Identity Theft and Pretext Calling | www.federalreserve.gov/boarddocs/SRLETTERS/2001/sr0111.htm |
| 11-00 | Guidance on the Risk Management of Outsourced Technology Services | www.federalreserve.gov/boarddocs/srletters/2000/sr0017.htm |

| Date | Title | URL |
|---|---|---|
| | Commercial Bank Examination Manual | Section 4060 revised to include the FFIEC interagency policy statement on the risk management of outsourced technology services.<br><br>www.federalreserve.gov/boarddocs/supmanual/default.htm#cbem |
| 02-00 | Outsourcing of Information and Transaction Processing | www.federalreserve.gov/boarddocs/SRLETTERS/2000/SR0004.HTM |
| 02-00 | Information Technology Examination Frequency | www.federalreserve.gov/boarddocs/SRLETTERS/2000/SR0003.HTM |
| 03-99 | Uniform Rating System for Information Technology | www.federalreserve.gov/boarddocs/SRLETTERS/1999/SR9908.HTM |
| 04-98 | Assessment of Information Technology in the Risk-Focused Frameworks for the Supervision of Community Banks and Large Complex Banking Organizations | www.federalreserve.gov/boarddocs/SRLETTERS/1998/SR9809.HTM |
| 02-98 | Management and Coordination of Information Technology for the Supervision Function | www.federalreserve.gov/boarddocs/srletters/1998/SR9801.HTM |
| 12-97 | Sound Practices for Information Security Networks | www.federalreserve.gov/boarddocs/SRLETTERS/1997/SR9732.HTM |
| 11-97 | Reporting of Computer Related Crimes by Financial Institutions | www.federalreserve.gov/boarddocs/SRLETTERS/1997/SR9728.HTM |
| 10-96 | Interagency Supervisory Statement on Risk Management of Client/Server Systems | www.federalreserve.gov/boarddocs/srletters/1996/sr9622.htm |

## National Credit Union Administration

| Date | Title | URL |
|------|-------|-----|
| 08-06 | NCUA Letter to Credit Unions 06-CU-13: Authentication for Internet Based Services | www.ncua.gov/letters/2006/CU/06-CU-13.pdf <br> www.ncua.gov/letters/2006/CU/06-CU-13_encl.pdf |
| 07-06 | NCUA Letter to Credit Unions 06-CU-12: Disaster Preparedness and Response Examination Procedures | www.ncua.gov/letters/2006/CU/06-CU-12.pdf |
| 06-06 | NCUA Letter to Credit Unions 06-CU-10: NCUA's Information System and Technology (IS&T) Program | www.ncua.gov/letters/2006/CU/06-CU-10.pdf <br> www.ncua.gov/letters/2006/CU/06-CU-10_Encl.pdf |
| 06-06 | NCUA Letter to Credit Unions 06-CU-11: Interagency Guidance Lessons Learned By Institutions Affected By Hurricane Katrina | www.ncua.gov/letters/2006/CU/06-CU-11.pdf <br> www.ncua.gov/Publications/brochures/LessonedLearned/Lessonslearned.pdf |
| 04-06 | NCUA Letter to Credit Unions 06-CU-07: IT Security Compliance Guide for Credit Unions | www.ncua.gov/letters/2006/CU/06-CU-07.pdf <br> www.ncua.gov/letters/2006/CU/06-CU-07Encl.pdf |
| 03-06 | NCUA Letter to Credit Unions 06-CU-06: Influenza Pandemic Preparedness | www.ncua.gov/letters/2006/CU/06-CU-06.pdf |
| 02-06 | NCUA Letter to Credit Unions 06-CU-01: Interagency Supervisory Guidance For Institutions Affected By Hurricane Katrina | www.ncua.gov/letters/2006/CU/06-CU-01.pdf <br> www.ncua.gov/letters/2006/CU/06-CU-01Enclosure.pdf |
| 09-04 | NCUA Letter to Credit Unions 04-CU-12: Phishing Guidance for Credit Union Members | www.ncua.gov/letters/2004/04-CU-12.pdf <br> www.ncua.gov/Publications/brochures/IdentityTheft/index.htm |
| 05-04 | NCUA Letter to Credit Unions 04-CU-06: E-Mail and Internet Related Fraudulent Schemes Guidance | www.ncua.gov/letters/2004/04-CU-06.pdf |
| 05-04 | NCUA Letter to Credit Unions 04-CU-05: Fraudulent E-Mail Schemes | www.ncua.gov/letters/2004/04-CU-05.pdf |
| 09-03 | NCUA Letter to Credit Unions 03-CU-14: Computer Software Patch Management | www.ncua.gov/letters/2003/03-CU-14.pdf <br> www.ncua.gov/letters/2003/03-CU-14Encl.pdf |

| Date | Title | URL |
|---|---|---|
| 08-03 | NCUA Letter to Credit Unions 03-CU-12: Fraudulent Newspaper Advertisements, and Websites by Entities Claiming to be Credit Unions | www.ncua.gov/letters/2003/03-CU-12.pdf |
| 04-03 | NCUA Letter to Credit Unions 03-CU-08: Weblinking: Identifying Risks and Risk Management Techniques | www.ncua.gov/letters/2003/03-CU-08.pdf |
| 03-03 | NCUA Letter to Credit Unions 03-CU-03: Wireless Technology | www.ncua.gov/letters/2003/03-CU-03.pdf |
| 12-02 | e-Commerce Guide for Credit Unions | www.ncua.gov/letters/2002/02-CU-17.htm<br><br>www.ncua.gov/letters/2002/02-CU-17EnclosureECommerceGuide.pdf |
| 07-02 | NCUA Letter to Credit Unions 02-CU-13: Vendor Information Systems and Technology Reviews: Summary Results | www.ncua.gov/letters/2002/02-CU-13.pdf |
| 07-02 | NCUA Letter to Federal Credit Unions 02-FCU-11: Tips to Safely Conduct Financial Transactions over the Internet: An NCUA Brochure for Credit Union Members | www.ncua.gov/letters/2002/02-FCU-11.pdf |
|  | AIRES Check Lists | www.ncua.gov/CreditUnionResources/aires/aires.html |
| 04-02 | NCUA Letter to Credit Unions 02–CU–08: Account Aggregation Services | www.ncua.gov/letters/2002/02-CU-08.pdf |
| 03-02 | NCUA Letter to Federal Credit Unions 02–FCU–04: Weblinking Relationships | www.ncua.gov/letters/2002/02-FCU-04.pdf |
| 12-01 | NCUA Letter to Credit Unions 01-CU-21: Disaster Recovery and Business Resumption Contingency Plans | www.ncua.gov/letters/2001/01-CU-21.pdf |
| 11-01 | NCUA Letter to Credit Unions 01-CU-20: Due Diligence Over Third-Party Service Providers | www.ncua.gov/letters/2001/01-CU-20.pdf |
| 10-01 | NCUA Letter to Credit Unions 01-CU-12: E-Commerce Insurance Considerations | www.ncua.gov/letters/2001/01-CU-12.pdf |

| Date | Title | URL |
|---|---|---|
| 09-01 | NCUA Letter to Credit Unions 01-CU-09: Identity Theft and Pretext Calling | www.ncua.gov/letters/2001/01-CU-09.pdf |
| 08-01 | NCUA Letter to Credit Unions 01-CU-11: Electronic Data Security Overview | www.ncua.gov/letters/2001/01-CU-11.pdf |
| 08-01 | NCUA Letter to Credit Unions 01-CU-10: Authentication in an Electronic Banking Environment | www.ncua.gov/letters/2001/01-CU-10.pdf |
| 03-01 | NCUA Regulatory Alert 01-RA-03: Electronic Signatures in Global and National Commerce Act (E-Sign Act) | www.ncua.gov/reg_alerts/Prior2003/01-RA-03.pdf |
| 02-01 | NCUA Letter to Credit Unions 01-CU-02: Privacy of Consumer Financial In-formation | www.ncua.gov/letters/2001/01-CU-02.pdf |
| 12-02 | e-Commerce Guide for Credit Unions | www.ncua.gov/letters/2002/02-CU-17.htm<br><br>www.ncua.gov/letters/2002/02-CU-17EnclosureECommerceGuide.pdf |
| 12-00 | NCUA Letter to Credit Unions 00-CU-11: Risk Management of Outsourced Technology Services (with Enclosure) | www.ncua.gov/letters/2000/00-CU-11.pdf |
| 10-00 | NCUA Letter to Credit Unions 00-CU-07: NCUA's Information Systems and Technology Examination Program | www.ncua.gov/letters/2000/00-CU-07.pdf |
| 07-00 | Suspicious Activity Report | www.ncua.gov/GuidesManuals/sar/sar.html |
|  | Privacy of Consumer Financial Information: Small Credit Union Compliance Guide | www.ncua.gov/ConsumerInformation/consumer_privacy/smallcucomplianceguide.pdf |
| 06-00 | NCUA Letter to Credit Unions 00-CU-04: Suspicious Activity Reporting (see section on "Computer Intrusion") | www.ncua.gov/letters/2000/00-CU-04.pdf |
| 05-00 | NCUA Letter to Credit Unions 00-CU-02: Identity Theft Prevention | www.ncua.gov/letters/2000/00-CU-02.pdf |

| Date | Title | URL |
|---|---|---|
| 02-99 | NCUA Regulatory Alert 99-RA-3: Pretext Phone Calling by Account Information Brokers | www.ncua.gov/reg_alerts/Prior2003/99-RA-3.pdf |
| 07-98 | NCUA Regulatory Alert 9-RA-4: Interagency Guidance on Electronic Financial Services and Consumer Compliance | www.ncua.gov/reg_alerts/Prior2003/98-ra-4.pdf |
| 04-97 | NCUA Letter to Credit Unions 97–CU–5: Interagency Statement on Retail On-Line PC Banking | www.ncua.gov/letters/1997/97-CU-5.html |
| 01-97 | NCUA Letter to Credit Unions 97-CU-1: Automated Response System Controls (January 1997) | www.ncua.gov/letters/1997/97-CU-1.html |
| 09-89 | NCUA Letter to Credit Unions 109: Information Processing Issues | www.ncua.gov/letters/Prior1996/e-let109.html |

## Office of the Comptroller of the Currency

| Date | Title | URL |
|---|---|---|
| 09-06 | Customer Authentication and Internet Banking Alert | www.occ.treas.gov/ftp/alert/2006-50.html |
| 09-06 | Automated Clearing House Activities: Risk Management Guidance | www.occ.treas.gov/ftp/bulletin/2006-39.pdf |
| 06-06 | Disaster Planning: Hurricane Katrina: Lessons Learned | www.occ.treas.gov/ftp/bulletin/2006-26.doc |
| 03-06 | Influenza Pandemic Preparedness | www.occ.treas.gov/ftp/bulletin/2006-12.doc |
| 10-05 | Authentication in an Internet Banking Environment | www.occ.treas.gov/netbank/ebguide.htm |
| 07/05 | Threats from Fraudulent Bank Web Sites: Risk Mitigation and Response Guidance for Web Site Spoofing Incidents | www.occ.treas.gov/ftp/bulletin/2005-24.doc |
| 4/05 | Response Programs for Unauthorized Access to Customer Information and Customer Notice: Final Guidance | www.occ.treas.gov/ftp/bulletin/2005-13.doc |

| Date | Title | URL |
|---|---|---|
| 05-04 | Risk Management of New, Expanded, or Modified Bank Products and Services | www.occ.treas.gov/ftp/bulletin/2004-20.doc |
| 06-04 | Electronic Record Keeping | www.occ.treas.gov/ftp/advisory/2004-9.doc |
| 05-04 | Payroll Card Systems | www.occ.treas.gov/ftp/advisory/2004-6.doc |
| 01-04 | Fictitious Emails to Financial Institutions Customers | www.occ.treas.gov/ftp/alert/2004-2.doc |
| 12-03 | Risk Management of Wireless Networks | www.occ.treas.gov/ftp/advisory/2003-10.txt |
| 07-03 | Community Bank Supervision | www.occ.gov/handbook/cbsh2003intro.pdf |
| 07-02 | Children's Online Privacy Protection Act (COPPA) | www.occ.treas.gov/ftp/bulletin/2002-31.doc |
| 05-02 | Electronic Banking Final Rule | www.occ.treas.gov/ftp/bulletin/2002-23.txt |
| 05-02 | Banks Use of Foreign Third-Party Service Providers | www.occ.treas.gov/ftp/bulletin/2002-16.doc |
| 01-02 | ACH Transactions Involving the Internet | www.occ.treas.gov/ftp/bulletin/2002-2.doc |
| 10-01 | Business Continuity and Security | Not publicly available |
| 07-01 | Examination Procedures to Evaluate Compliance with the Guidelines to Safeguard Customer Information | www.occ.treas.gov/fty/bulletin/2001-35.doc |
|  | Examination Procedures | www.occ.treas.gov/ftp/bulletin/2001-35a.pdf |
|  | Information Technology Portion of draft Community Bank Supervision booklet | www.occ.treas.gov/ftp/bulletin/2001-35b.pdf |
| 11/01 | Third-Party Relationships: Risk Management Principles | www.occ.treas.gov/ftp/bulletin/2001-47.doc |
| 07-01 | Weblinking: Message to Bankers and Examiners | www.occ.treas.gov/ftp/bulletin/2001-31.doc |

| Date | Title | URL |
|---|---|---|
| 05-01 | Privacy of Consumer Financial Information | www.occ.treas.gov/ftp/bulletin/2001-26.doc |
| 05-01 | Large Bank Supervision | www.occ.gov/handbook/lbs.pdf |
| 04-01 | Identity Theft and Pretext Calling | www.occ.treas.gov/ftp/advisory/2001-4.doc |
| 04-01 | Network Security Vulnerabilities | www.occ.treas.gov/ftp/alert/2001-4.doc |
| 02-01 | Bank Provided Aggregation Services | www.occ.treas.gov/ftp/bulletin/2001-12.doc |
| 01-01 | Corporate Manual on Internet Banking | www.occ.treas.gov/corpbook/group4/public/pdf/internet nbc.pdf |
| 01-01 | Internet-Initiated ACH Debits/ACH Risk | www.occ.treas.gov/ftp/advisory/2001-3.doc |
| 09-00 | Privacy Laws and Regulations | www.occ.treas.gov/ftp/bulletin/2000-25a.pdf |
| 07-00 | Protecting Internet Addresses of National Banks | www.occ.treas.gov/ftp/alert/2000-9.txt |
| 05-00 | Infrastructure Threats: Intrusion Risks | www.occ.treas.gov/ftp/bulletin/2000-14.txt |
| 02-00 | Internet Security: Distributed Denial of Service Attacks | www.occ.treas.gov/ftp/alert/2000-1.txt |
| 05-99 | Guidance to National Banks on Web Site Privacy Statements | www.occ.treas.gov/ftp/advisory/99-6.txt |
| 05-99 | Certification Authority Systems for Digital Signatures | www.occ.treas.gov/ftp/bulletin/99-20.txt |
| 02-98 | Technology Risk Management – Guidance for Bankers / Examiners | www.occ.teras.gov/ftp/bulletin/98-3.txt |
| 09-96 | Stored Value Card Systems – Information for Bankers / Examiners | www.occ/treas.gov/ftp/bulletin/96-48.txt |
| 05-95 | Management Information Systems Booklet | (out of print) |

## Summary of Regulatory Guidance on Electronic Banking and Information Technology Basel Committee on Banking Supervision: Available online at www.bis.org/publ

| Date | Title | URL |
|---|---|---|
| 04-03 | The New Basel Capital Accord: Third Consultative Paper | www.bis.org/bcbs/bcbscp3.htm |
| 12-01 | The New Basel Capital Accord | www.bis.org/publ/bcbsca.htm |
| 10-00 | Electronic Banking Group Initiatives and Papers | www.bis.org/publ/bcbs76.htm |
| 03-98 | Risk Management for Electronic Banking and Electronic Money Activities | www.bis.org/publ/bcbs35.htm |

## Office of Federal Housing Enterprise Oversight

| Date | Title | URL |
|---|---|---|
| 11-06 | OFHEO Examination Guidance for Corporate Governance | www.ofheo.gov/media/pdf/corpgovguidance11806.pdf |
| 12-01 | OFHEO Policy Guidance on Safety and Soundness Standards for Information | www.ofheo.gov/media/pdf/pg01002.pdf |
| 12-00 | OFHEO Policy Guidance on Minimum Safety and Soundness Requirements | www.ofheo.gov/media/pdf/pg00001.pdf |

**Office of Thrift Supervision:** Most available online at: www.ots.treas.gov. See also Electronic Banking website at www.ots.treas.gov/ebanking.html.

| Date | Title | URL |
|---|---|---|
| 04-06 | Examination Handbook | Section 341, Information Technology Risks and Controls. This section includes examination guidance and procedures for smaller, less complex savings associations. It contains examination guidance and procedures for the Interagency Guidelines Establishing Information Security Standards (Security Guidelines). The Security Guidelines, effective July 1, 2001, implement section 501(b) of the Gramm-Leach-Bliley Act (GLB Act). Guidance: www.ots.treas.gov/docs/4/422120.pdf Examination Procedures: www.ots.treas.gov/docs/4/422120.pdf |

| Date | Title | URL |
|------|-------|-----|
| 10-06 | Updated Director's Responsibility Guide and Guide to Management Reports | www.ots.treas.gov/docs/2/25245.pdf |
| Various | Examination Handbook | The comprehensive OTS Handbook that contains all safety and soundness and compliance examination guidance. This handbook addresses all major areas of concern in examinations of OTS-regulated savings associations. The handbook sections link to examination programs that contain examination objectives and procedures.<br><br>www.ots.treas.gov/da.cfm?catNumber=113&an=11 |
| 08-06 | Frequently Asked Questions on Authentication in an Internet Banking Environment | www.ots.treas.gov/docs/2/25242.pdf |
| 06-06 | Hurricane Katrina: Industry Lessons Learned | www.ots.treas.gov/docs/2/25239.pdf |
| 03-06 | Advisory on Influenza Pandemic Preparedness | www.ots.treas.gov/docs/2/25237.pdf |
| 12-05 | Compliance Guide for Information Security Standards | www.ots.treas.gov/docs/2/25231.pdf |
| 10-05 | Authentication in an Internet Banking Environment | www.ots.treas.gov/docs/2/25228.pdf |
| 03-05 | Response Programs for Unauthorized Access to Customer Information and Customer Notice: Final Guidance | www.ots.treas.gov/docs/2/25214.pdf |
| 08-03 | Request for Comment on Guidance for Response Programs for Unauthorized Access to Customer Information and Customer Notice | www.ots.treas.gov/docs/2/25179.pdf |
| 10-04 | Risk Management of Free and Open Source Software | www.ots.treas.gov/docs/2/25207.pdf |
| 09-04 | Third Party Arrangements | www.ots.treas.gov/docs/8/84272.pdf |
| 09-04 | "Phishing" Customer Brochure | www.ots.treas.gov/docs/2/25205.pdf |
| 03-04 | "Phishing" and Email Scams | www.ots.treas.gov/docs/2/25193.pdf |

| Date | Title | URL |
|---|---|---|
| 04-03 | Interagency Guidance on Weblinking: Identifying Risks and Risk Techniques | www.ots.treas.gov/docs/8/84263.pdf |
| 03-03 | Interagency Policy Statement on Internal Audit Function and its Outsourcing | www.ots.treas.gov/docs/8/84260.pdf |
| 05-01 | Identity Theft and Pretext Calling | www.ots.treas.gov/docs/2/25139.pdf |
| 06-99 | Transactional Web sites | www.ots.treas.gov/docs/2/25109.pdf |
| 11-98 | Policy Statement on Pretext Calling | www.ots.treas.gov/docs/2/25097.pdf |
| 11-98 | Policy Statement on Privacy and Accuracy of Customer Information | www.ots.treas.gov/docs/2/25097.pdf |
| 12-97 | Guidance Concerning Reporting of Computer-Related Crimes | www.ots.treas.gov/docs/2/25075.pdf |

## Guidance and Key Documents: State Regulators

### Conference of State Bank Supervisors

| Date | Title | URL |
|---|---|---|
| 11-96 | Nationwide State-Federal Supervisory Agreement | www.csbs.org/Content/NavigationMenu/RegulatoryAffairs/ SupervisoryAgreementsApplications/nationwide_state_fed_ supervisory_agrmnt.pdf |
| 12-97 | Nationwide Cooperative Agreement | www.csbs.org/Content/NavigationMenu/RegulatoryAffairs/ SupervisoryAgreementsApplications/nationwide_coop_agrmnt.pdf |
| 11-98 | Nationwide State Foreign Bank Office (FBO) Agreement | www.csbs.org/Content/NavigationMenu/RegulatoryAffairs/ SupervisoryAgreementsApplications/state_fbo_agrmnt.pdf |
| 11-98 | Nationwide State-Federal Foreign Bank Office (FBO) Agreement | www.csbs.org/Content/NavigationMenu/RegulatoryAffairs/ SupervisoryAgreementsApplications/state_federal_fbo_agrmnt.pdf |

| Date | Title | URL |
|---|---|---|
| | Nationwide Cooperative Agreement for the Supervision and Examination of Multi-State Trust Institutions (Nationwide Trust Agreement) | www.csbs.org/Content/NavigationMenu/RegulatoryAffairs/SupervisoryAgreementsApplications/nationwide_agrmnt_multi-state_trust_op.pdf |
| | CSBS Statutory Options for Multi-State Trust Activities | www.csbs.org/Content/NavigationMenu/RegulatoryAffairs/SupervisoryAgreementsApplications/model_trust_law.pdf |
| | State/Federal Supervisory Protocol | www.csbs.org/Content/NavigationMenu/RegulatoryAffairs/SupervisoryAgreementsApplications/StateFederalSupervisoryProtocol.pdf |

# Appendix 3: FSSCC Research and Development Agenda

**Research Agenda – September 30, 2006 Draft**

## 1. Background

The Department of Homeland Security (DHS) recently published its National Infrastructure Protection Plan (NIPP). The NIPP states that academic and research center communities play an important role in enabling national-level critical infrastructure and key resources (CI/KR) protection and implementation of the NIPP (section 2.2.7). This plan states the intention of DHS to examine existing cyber security programs within the research and academic communities to determine their applicability as models for critical infrastructure protection education and broad-based research (section 6.2). Further, it articulates strategic research and development (R&D) goals and identifies the R&D areas in which advances in CI/KR protection must be made. It describes specific R&D plans and programs that support the NIPP (section 6.3 and appendix 6).

In 2003, the President released the National Strategy to Secure Cyberspace and *National Strategy for Physical Protection of Critical Infrastructures and Key Assets*. These documents called for Treasury, as the sector lead agency for the Banking and Finance Sector, to develop a R&D agenda for the sector. Treasury, working with the Financial and Banking Information Infrastructure Committee (FBIIC) and the Financial Services Sector Coordinating Council (FSSCC), published research challenges for the sector entitled *Closing the Gap*. The driving force behind the document was a desire to identify key areas where additional research dollars could be spent to make the sector more secure. This document, released in 2003, was socialized among Federal departments and agencies, academics, and financial services participants.

As the issue of R&D for the financial services sector matured, the FSSCC developed a working group to focus specifically on the issue for R&D and to coordinate its activities with respect to CI/KR R&D. At the request of Treasury, the FSSCC joined DHS in a May 2005 workshop focused on R&D priorities. As DHS was finalizing the NIPP R&D plans and programs, the FSSCC formed an R&D Committee to focus on those plans and programs that would provide the most significant benefits with respect to the specific CI/KR requirements of the financial services industry. In May 2006, this committee issued a list of research projects that provide information security professionals with tools to address known vulnerabilities in the financial services industry, titled *The FSSCC Research and Development Committee Research Challenges*.

This document was not written to reproduce either the NIPP or FSSCC R&D document, but rather it is intended to enable an academic researcher, a DHS reviewer, or other interested reader to determine quickly the applicability of an FSSCC R&D challenge to a given NIPP R&D theme, plan, or program.

## 2. Objective

The objective of this paper is to demonstrate how FSSCC research challenges relate to the NIPP R&D plans and programs, as well as to demonstrate the aspects in which they differ. Because this paper combines the opinions of subject matter experts in homeland security and financial services, the resulting recommendations will meet the needs of both constituencies. It is intended that DHS should use this information to tweak its projects to directly address the CI/KR research needs of the financial services industry. Consequently, the future direction and scope of the NIPP research program will align more closely with the proposed FSSCC research challenge. For example, in the next version of the NIPP, DHS may add new R&D areas of focus that are in the FSSCC document but are not in the current NIPP. In addition, they may be included in the financial services sector-specific infrastructure protection plan.

The FSSCC understands that all sectors have been requested to share their R&D plan with DHS to facilitate similar gap analyses across sectors. Were all sectors to perform gap analyses similar to that of this document, it would be easier for DHS to align its overall R&D program with the needs of other sectors as well. The FSSCC is committed to participating in any activity that renders a DHS R&D program that is consistent across sectors, between critical sectors, and the overall NIPP program.

## 3. Approach

The 2006 NIPP approach to conducting research and development and using technology is described section 6.3 of the NIPP. It highlights three areas of planning and program activities that are intended to allocate protection resources where they can best mitigate risk: (1) the NIPP R&D Plan, (2) the Federal Plan for Cyber Security R&D, and (3) R&D and planning efforts conducted by the Sector-Specific Agencies (SSAs). This FSSCC research agenda identifies challenges that are the central focus of R&D and planning efforts conducted by the financial services SSA, the Department of the Treasury. This document compares the FSSCC research challenges to the overall NIPP R&D program.

Central to this comparison is a matrix (see appendix A) that shows the relationship between the FSSCC R&D research challenges items and the NIPP R&D program. The matrix is intended to demonstrate that choosing a financial industry R&D challenge item as a focus area for research in pursuit of NIPP R&D goals will provide research opportunities that are both well-defined and fertile. The rows of the matrix identify the eight FSSCC R&D challenges. Most of the columns of the table show the areas of research promulgated in the NIPP. The last four columns are R&D areas contemplated in the FSSCC program but not included in the NIPP.

Columns labeled A-I are headed with NIPP themes (described in section 6.3.3.2 and appendix 6). Columns labeled J-M are labeled with other NIPP R&D areas (described in section 6.5 and appendix 6). Columns labeled N-Q are labeled with financial sector technology requirements for R&D (referred to in section 6.3.3.4) that are not R&D focus areas in the current NIPP. Where there is a letter in the cell at the intersection of an FSSCC research challenge and an R&D area, it is meant to assert that a focus on the FSSCC research challenge as a subject of research in the corresponding NIPP R&D area would provide immediate benefit to the Banking and Finance Sector. Because the benefit would be a well-defined measure of success in the R&D effort, such benefit would facilitate problem solving not only in the financial services industry, but also in any industry that requires progress in that R&D area to solve its own problems. In each case, a brief statement of the reason for this assertion is included in the "Research Guidance" section that follows the matrix. The guidance in that section identifies the focus area of intersection between the FSSCC research challenge and the NIPP R&D area listed in the column heading. That is, the note labeled with the letter in the cell corresponding to the R&D area for which the FSSCC research challenge should be a subject of the intersecting NIPP R&D area focus is meant to convey the benefit of using the FSSCC research challenge as a focus area for that research area.

In addition, R&D focus on the eight FSSCC research challenges will help contribute to, and benefit from, the attainment of the NIPP R&D long-term strategic goals, namely:

1. Common operating picture architecture;

2. Next-generation Internet with built-in security; and

3. Resilient, self-diagnosing, self-healing systems.

These goals will be achieved in the financial services industry only in conjunction with commensurate advances in CI/KR technology. These advances will be achieved only if steady focus is maintained on the financial industry R&D challenges.

## 4. Research Guidance

This guidance explains why R&D in the FSSCC research challenge is a good and proper area of focus for R&D in the area corresponding to the lettered column of the NIPP columns (A-M) of the matrix. For example, paragraph B in section 4.1 below is meant to be understood as:

> Secure Financial Transaction Protocol (SFTP) R&D is a good and proper area of focus for R&D in the area of protection and prevention systems because protection and prevention systems are needed to protect against abuses of batch and real-time transaction processing capabilities and to prevent certain fraudulent transactions from being processed.

This guidance also explains why the FSSCC R&D Committee has proposed four categories of R&D plans and programs that are not addressed specifically in the NIPP. It describes why R&D focused on FSSCC research challenges will need to concentrate some effort on the more general R&D theme identified (in columns N-Q of the matrix). For example, the paragraph Q in section 4.1 below is to be understood as:

> R&D focused on SFTP requires as a prerequisite some focus on the "Economics of InfoSec" because the widespread acceptance of the results of SFTP research will rely on the development of an economic model for secure communications types. This is because the costs to implement and maintain SFTP must not present an unacceptable burden to smaller merchants or local banks that may operate with limited technical expertise and lower budgets.

The format of each guidance paragraph is abbreviated because it is not intended to reproduce either the NIPP or FSSCC research challenge document, but rather is intended to enable an academic researcher, a DHS reviewer, or other interested reader to determine quickly the applicability of the FSSCC research challenge to a larger NIPP or other research area field of study.

### 4.1 Secure Financial Transaction Protocol (SFTP)

**B**   Protection and prevention systems are needed to protect against abuses of batch and real-time transaction processing capabilities and to prevent impersonation-enabled fraudulent transactions from being processed.

**H**   Advanced infrastructure architectures are required to assure that availability and resiliency demands for SFTP are met. This includes non-stop processing and intelligent distributed systems designs to achieve agreed-upon service levels.

**J**   Compatibility of communications systems with interoperability standards is a must for any SFTP to assure that, regardless of the sender's computing resources, transactions can be interpreted and processed successfully.

**K**   SFTP requires that mutual authentication of parties is established prior to transaction processing. Both automated and human-interactive operations are in scope.

**L**   SFTP, as well as any other secure protocols that accomplish NIPP R&D programs, should utilize and thus benefit from rigorous acceptance methodology, including submittal to the ANSI X9 Committee for ratification and eventual certification by the International Organization for Standardization (ISO) for Finance and Banking Standards.

**N**    R&D focused on SFTP will require effort to develop information-hiding techniques because they are needed to protect sensitive customer and confidential information from unauthorized access while avoiding more onerous or unmanageable cryptographic practices. (A related requirement is that key management needs to be simple, secure, and transparent.)

**Q**    R&D focused on SFTP will require effort to develop economic models for secure communication methods because costs to implement and maintain SFTP must not present an unacceptable burden to smaller merchants or local banks that may operate with limited technical expertise and lower budgets.

## 4.2 Resilient Financial Transaction System (RFTS)

**B, C, & F**    A distributed, resilient financial system must use best practices to prevent damage or destruction, including restricting entry and access to physical infrastructure. Research and practices in those areas could be applied to any infrastructure with high reliability and resiliency requirements. The distributed environment could be used to house detection and sensor systems and to disseminate the information those sensors carry, to aid in the system's self-healing capabilities.

**E**    Automated decision-support and analysis are a subcomponent of any resultant transaction system. Increases in online fraud have made the financial industry fertile ground for such real-time analysis.

**H**    As the financial industry becomes more and more automated, financial systems technology architects and engineers require access to research in the design of complex systems, including modeling, operation, and failure-recovery.

**I**    Government and private sector coordination during a terrorist attack and risk communication and management will be key areas for maintaining CI/KR to support a functioning financial sector during a natural or manmade disaster. Models developed in this area would apply broadly to other CI/KR sectors.

**L**    The processes, standards, and procedures developed to run such a system would be applicable to other systems with similar scope and resiliency requirements.

## 4.3 Enrollment and Identity Credential Management

**B, H, & K**    The necessary improvements in enrollment and identity credential systems require advances in protection and prevention systems, development of advanced infrastructure architectures, and advanced methods to authenticate and verify personal identity to meet the performance objectives.

**I**    Improvements in financial systems customer enrollment, data consumption, and aggregation habits require greater knowledge of human and social issues. Decisions that financial services customers make with respect to personal privacy and convenience are both appropriate and well-defined topics for research.

## 4.4 Suggested Practices and Standards

**A, B**    The financial sector is the most common target of miscreants' activity due to the potential for financial gain. The sector is subject to constant attack, both traditional and innovative. Hence, it is a most fertile field for research on detection and sensor systems, and the sector also has been a leader in combining detection with prevention, as potential fraud activity triggers additional control. Research results in layering these technologies easily could be ported to the requirements of other industries.

**C**    Due to the FDIC guidance with respect to two-factor authentication, the financial sector has established cooperative efforts devoted to entry and access portals. Researchers in these areas are encouraged to contact the Financial Services Technology Consortium (FSTC) to learn more about them and to join and contribute to these efforts through the Object Management Group (OMG), Open Web Application Security Project (OWASP) and other standards groups where financial institutions' members are very active. One of the subsets or measurable outcomes can be particular to the financial sector, but the modeling needs to take into account the interdependence of all sectors.

**D**  The financial sector has adopted practices from the retail sector and is, through BITS, establishing a database of offenders to be used to protect financial institutions from undue harm. Commonalities in the use of such information across sectors would benefit the implementation of practices and standards and could lead to acceptable use criteria for such information. This could lead to a possible profiling tool that could be used as a model across all industries.

**E**  Critical infrastructure protection decision support and analysis systems are not unique to the financial sector, but inter-sector and intra-sector dependence needs to be analyzed in order for the financial sector to make use of them. The financial sector would make a good starting point for such research as the sector firmly grasps success criteria and measurable outcomes. These criteria can be particular to the financial sector, while the modeling takes into account the interdependence of all sectors.

**F**  Financial services regulators commonly have been vague with respect to recovery standards (e.g., "no single event can impact your ability to do business.") No central source for practices and standards takes into account uptime requirements, data transmission limitations, and the limitations of the Nation's critical infrastructure. As the financial sector has business continuity planning (BCP) requirements that span dependence on other sectors, it is logical that research into standards that meet those requirements be done within the sector. The benefits then can be drawn by other industries that may not have as much of a regulatory mandate but still could benefit from standards for calculating the present value of BCP and recovery efforts.

**G**  Emerging threats are by definition unknown, but as vulnerabilities become known, threats commonly are enacted first against the financial sector. It is imminently important for institutions in the financial sector to be able to find out quickly about threats, to assess their possible impact, and to react. Research into standards for making best use of centrally identified emerging threats would be invaluable to the financial sector and a model that could be carried easily to other industries.

**H**  The financial sector has long been the main driver for security features in vendor products aimed at advanced infrastructure architecture. Research, development, implementation, and creation of guidelines for any advanced infrastructure within the financial sector would make best use of the embedded knowledge base in financial services while promoting secure, self-healing, interoperable, and redundant systems that then could be used in all industries that utilize the Internet.

**I**  Human and social issues can affect all industries. But not all industries are considered critical to how we function as a society. Human and social issues need to be factored into the continuity plans of critical areas such as the financial sector. For example, the impact of mass absenteeism due to a pandemic can affect our financial fabric and could be examined, modeled, promulgated, and factored into all continuity planning.

**J**  Establishing data transmission interoperability standards for the financial sector would enable banking and clearing operations to continue seamlessly. This would aid in enhancing public confidence in our financial sector and would be reusable for other industries.

**K**  The establishment of standards and protocols based on new and best practices for identification and authentication would help all industries that engage in transactions that involve two or more parties. The financial sector is an especially rich area for this research due to the large volume of transactions and their susceptibility to fraud.

**L**  The financial services sector is wholly committed to the establishment of CI/KR protection consensus standards, and inter- and intra-dependence of the financial sector with other sectors should be considered.

**M**  The NIPP detection and sensor systems may be considered to include cyber surveillance. Although the use of Intrusion Detection Systems (IDS) and Intrusion Prevention Systems (IPS) in the financial sector is commonplace, there is no common set of guidelines that would be applicable to most situations. The ability to establish such a document could be easily adapted to other industries.

**N** The financial sector is an especially good area for a test due to the large volume of transactions and their susceptibility to fraud. For example, use of a stenographic technique within the data transfer to identify a user will enhance identity management benefiting all industries in the short term.

**O** Where security vulnerabilities present challenges, the only option so far available to the financial sector is to discontinue service. Research into the motivation for targeting certain financial services and institutions may enable the financial sector and other industries to develop methods for devaluing services.

**P** Simulation is key to predicting the impact of vulnerabilities and protective measures. Financial service simulation is relatively easy to accomplish as physical resources generally are not required. Yet research into business process simulation may benefit all industries.

**Q** There is currently a distinct inability to rationalize spending additional money on information security due to the lack of data on the impact of threats enacted due to vulnerabilities that could have been avoided. There is therefore a lack of any standardized return on investment calculation. Such research could benefit all industries that employ information security tools and techniques.

## 4.5 Understanding and Avoiding the Insider Threat

**B, D, M** Prevention and protection of assets from trusted insiders need to capitalize on automatic mechanisms that enforce dual controls, separation of duties, role-based permissions, and configuration controls that can detect, alert, and respond to attempts of installing rogue software in production systems.

**I** Financial institutions have numerous case studies and scenarios where motivation combined with opportunity result in fraud. Research in human and social issues should be targeted at reducing the motivation quotient of the fraud equation.

**I** Financial institutions provide corrupt insiders with financial motivation. Research into methods of devaluing assets upon detection of insider manipulation may serve to reduce this threat.

**G** Automation of mechanisms to detect potential malicious activity or escalation of privileges are required for all computing resources, including end-user PCs and laptops attached to corporate networks.

## 4.6 Financial Information Tracing and Policy Enforcement

**B** Financial information policy enforcement would benefit from advances in prevention systems with respect to real-time information sharing on known fraud issues to block transactions.

**E** Financial information policy enforcement would benefit from research into decision support with respect to terrorist economic activity.

**G** Financial information tracing would benefit from research into emerging threats to an individual's financial status and vulnerability analysis aids.

**H** As infrastructure architectures become more advanced, a constant focus on policy enforcement will be required to identify the infrastructure component upon which a given compute operation depends. A focus on rigorous and concrete regulatory logging requirements will provide detailed requirements for those research activities.

**I** Human and social issues are key to policy enforcement and focus on accountability, and the level of traceability requested to establish it with respect to financial transactions will serve to establish criteria for success in influencing behavior.

**K**  Financial information tracing is not possible unless the identity of the transaction initiator is able to be carried through the multiple layer of authentication required to navigate through complex infrastructure.

**M**  Financial transaction anomaly detection R&D in private financial institutions has set the bar for advances in technical surveillance, monitoring, and detection.

**P**  Reference to potential threats to the stability of the economic infrastructure often cite inability to trace financial transactions, and business process simulation of this domain would serve to mitigate this and similar online identity-related threats.

**Q**  The ability to trace a financial transaction to an accountable source is key to the easiest demonstration of the economics of InfoSec: antifraud measures. Moreover, the methodology of tracing accountability is extensible to other sectors.

## 4.7 Testing

**B**  Improving the quality of software and providing proven guidelines for organizations to use for software certification can improve the defensive posture of CI/KR with software-based components. Such research can also provide near-term security and economic benefits for the financial and other industries that rely heavily on software process automation.

**G**  Many new attacks are the result of exploiting a newly-discovered software bug before a patch can be applied. Higher-quality software testing and certification can help reduce the number of emerging threats against CI/KR.

**H**  A new, more secure architecture, while desirable, discards the years of real-world experience with current system deployments. Rigorous software testing standards will be necessary to ensure a new architecture does not initially weaken systems' defensive posture.

**L**  Software testing and certification standards can help coordinate work and provide a shared yardstick for measuring posture cross-sector. Financial industry problems are good barometers of succession because validation of tests results is of paramount importance where dollars are involved.

## 4.8 Standards for measuring ROI of CIP and Security Technology

**E, G, I, Q**  Individual organizations in the public and private sectors tend to optimize locally with respect to investing in critical infrastructure protection rather than talking a global perspective. Economic and capital budgeting models need to be developed which assist in determining the global impact of security-related decisions. Such models should be the basis for determining the optimal expenditures, which will yield the highest global ROI, for all the other Challenge Projects. Researchers need to first determine the components to be included in such a global ROI calculation and then provide suitable methods for analyzing them in the context of R&D funding decision-making.

## 5. Conclusions and Recommendations

It is apparent from the above analysis that there are many areas common to both proposed research programs and that, with minor modifications, the two programs can be synchronized to mutual benefit. Especially noteworthy are the following National R&D themes that, as depicted in the comparison matrix, would seem to have the most impact to the Financial Services Sector:

- Protection and Prevention Systems (matrix column B);

- Advanced Infrastructure Architecture (matrix column H); and

- Human and Social Issues (matrix column I).

The FSSCC R&D committee recommends that research in these areas be given national priority. We stand ready to assist in developing a coordinated plan through the Department of Treasury and between critical sectors, and the overall NIPP Program.

Table A-1: Comparison Matrix: FSSCC R&D Challenges vs. NIPP R&D Themes

| FSSCC Research Challenge | NIPP CI/KR Protection R&D Themes | | | | | | | | | Other R&D Support for CI/KR | | | | Items not in NIPP R&D Focus | | | |
|---|---|---|---|---|---|---|---|---|---|---|---|---|---|---|---|---|---|
| | A Detection & Sensor Systems | B Protection & Prevention Systems | C Entry & Access Portals | D Insider Threat Detection | E Analysis & Decision Support Systems | F Response, Recovery, & Reconstitution Tools | G Emerging Threats & Vulnerability Analysis Aids | H Advanced Infrastructure Architectures | I Human & Social Issues | J Ensure compatibility of communication systems with inter-operability standards | K Explore methods to authenticate and verify personal identity | L Coordinate development of CI/KR protection consensus standards | M Improve technical surveillance, monitoring, and detection capabilities | N Information Hiding | O Devaluation and Avoidance | P Business Process Simulation | Q Economics of InfoSec |
| 1. Secure Financial Transaction Protocol (SFTP) | | B | | | | | | H | | J | K | L | | N | | | Q |
| 2. Resilient Financial Transaction System (RFTS) | | B | C | | | F | | H | I | | | L | | | | | |
| 3. Enrollment and Identity Credential Management | | B | | | | | | H | I | | K | | | | | | |
| 4. Suggested Practices and Standards | A | B | C | D | E | F | G | H | I | J | K | L | M | N | O | P | Q |
| 5. Understanding and Avoiding the Insider Threat | A | B | | D | | | G | | I | | | | M | | | | |
| 6. Financial Information Tracing and Policy Enforcement | | B | | | E | | G | H | I | | K | | M | N | | P | Q |
| 7. Testing | | B | | | | | G | H | | | | L | | | | | |
| 8. Standards for Measuring ROI of CIP and Security Technology | | | | | E | | G | | I | | | | | | | | Q |

www.ingramcontent.com/pod-product-compliance
Lightning Source LLC
Chambersburg PA
CBHW080306290526
45790CB00005B/1951